HOW THE HELL...
DO I GET MY FILM FINANCED?

Book One: Tax Incentives

How Choosing The Right Location Can Help You Get Your Film Or TV Show Financed And Produced!

Part of the "HOW THE HELL..." series

Written by
Ricky Margolis

Published by
Wunderfunkmaschine

"HOW THE HELL... DO I GET MY FILM FINANCED? Book One: Tax Incentives : How Choosing The Right Location Can Help You Get Your Film Or TV Show Financed And Produced!"
Part of the "HOW THE HELL..." series
Written by Ricky Margolis
Published by Wunderfunkmaschine LLC
Edited by Jasper Parks
Additional Editing by Sean Mandell
Cover Design by Wunderfunkmaschine
Print Edition ISBN: 978-1-952495-02-1
E-Book Edition ISBN: 978-1-952495-00-7
For further information, please e-mail us at info@wunderfunkmaschine.com, or visit us at our website at www.wunderfunkmaschine.com.

Copyright © 2020 Richard "Ricky" Margolis
The moral rights of the author have been asserted.
All rights reserved. No part of this book may be reproduced, stored in a retrieval system or transmitted in any form or by any means electronic, mechanical, photocopying, recording or otherwise without the prior written permission of the publisher.
The information provided in this book is for informational purposes only and is not intended to be a source of advice of any kind, including but not necessarily limited to investment advice or tax advice, with respect to the material presented. The author is not a licensed or accredited professional in the fields discussed in this book. The information and/or documents contained in this book do not constitute legal or financial advice and should never be used without first consulting with an appropriate professional in the relevant field to determine what may be best for your individual needs. No decisions regarding either investing or raising money should be made based solely on the information contained in this book.

The publisher and the author do not make any guarantee or other promise as to any results that may be obtained from using the content of this book, which is no substitute for direct expert assistance which should be sought if necessary. You should never make any investment decision without first consulting with your own financial advisor and conducting your own research and due diligence. It is your responsibility to comply with the necessary rules and regulations set forth by your governing jurisdiction when raising and/or investing funds.

To the maximum extent permitted by law, the publisher and the author disclaim any and all liability in the event that any information, commentary, analysis, opinions, advice and/or recommendations contained in this book prove to be inaccurate, incomplete or unreliable. The publisher and the author disclaim any liability for any losses (investment or otherwise) or other consequences or impacts resulting directly or indirectly from the use of the information contained in this book. All data has been provided on a 'good faith' basis and every effort has been made to ensure that it is accurate at the time of publication, however the publisher and the author disclaim any liability should such information contained within the book prove not to be accurate.

Investing in the entertainment industry (including in films and television shows) can be highly risky and should only be done by sophisticated investors following the correct advice. Raising money in the entertainment industry (including in films and television shows) also carries certain risks and responsibilities. The publisher and the author are providing this book and its contents on an "as is" basis and make no representations or warranties of any kind with respect to the book's contents. Your use of the information in this book is at your own risk.

Table Of Contents

PART ONE 8

1. **What Is A Tax Incentive?** 9
2. **The Aims Of This Book** 11
   Who Is This Book For?... 12
   Not An Incentives Guide 12
3. **An Overview Of Tax Incentives** 15
   Production Hubs 15
   'Non-Traditional' Shooting Locations 16
   Consider All Options 17
4. **How Does A Tax Incentive Work?** 18
   Example 18
   Using The Incentive To Raise Production Financing............ 19
   A Sophisticated Landscape 19
5. **Do I Need to Know Anything About Tax?** 21
   Stimulating The Economy... 21
   Local Procedures 22
   Transparency... 23
   Stick To The Rules... 24
6. **Choosing Your Location** 25
   Start With The Creative 25
   How Do I Find Out About A Location's Tax Incentive?........ 26
7. **How Much Money Will A Tax Incentive Generate?** 28
   The Incentive As A Percentage 28
8. **Qualifying Spend** 30
   What Is Qualifying Spend? 30
   Which Items Can Be Included 31
   As Qualifying Spend?.. 31
   Analyzing The Legislation..32
   Different Ways Of Comparing This Information..................34
9. **Why Won't My Entire Budget Qualify For The Tax Incentive?** 37
   Development 37
   Post-Production, VFX And Delivery Costs 39
   ATL And BTL..42
   Resident Labor And Non-Resident Labor 45

10.	Calculating The Tax Incentive Value	48
	Example	48
	Assumptions	50
11.	Maximizing The Value Of Your Tax Incentive	51

PART TWO 53

12.	What Kinds of Tax Incentives Are There?	54
13.	**Tax Rebates**	**56**
	Basic Principles	56
	Case Study	57
14.	**Tax Credits**	**61**
	Basic Principles	61
	How To Use A Tax Credit	62
	But What If I Don't Pay Taxes In That Location?	63
	What Do I Do With My Tax Credit?	63
	Selling A Tax Credit	64
	Understanding Pricing	65
	How Much Is My Tax Credit Worth?	66
	Tax Credit Brokers	67
	Choosing A Broker	68
	Making A Deal With A Broker	69
	Broker Fees	71
	State Buy-Backs	71
	State Transferability	73
	Other Restrictions	73
	Case Study	75
	Next Steps	76
	Additional Costs	78
	A Little Extra Effort	79
15.	**Local Requirements**	**80**
	Pre-Certification	80
	Setting Up An SPV	82
	Audit	83
	Credits And Logo	84
	Content Review And Finished Product	84
	Distribution	86
	Minimum Requirements	87
	Caps	89
16.	**Local Infrastructure**	**93**
	Are There Enough Local Crews Available?	93
	Are The Crews Of A High Standard?	94

Are There Enough High-Quality Amenities To Suit Your
Needs? 95
Is There Enough Entertainment To Keep People Occupied On
Their Days Off? 96
Is There So Much Going On That They Will Be Distracted?. 97
Is It Safe? 98
Will All The Facilities You Need Be Available? 98
How Do You Deal With The Local Unions? 99

PART THREE **101**

   17.   **Now What?** **102**

   18.   **Cash-Flowing Your Tax Incentive** **104**
   What Does 'Cash-Flowing A Tax Incentive' Mean? 104
   Who Can Cash-Flow My Tax Incentive? 105
   How Much Does This Cost? 107
   Paying The Fees And Interest 108
   Interest Reserve 109
   Turnaround Time 109
   Late Fees And Penalties 110
   Legal Fees And Logistics 112
   Independent Analysis 113
   Discount 115
   Financial Closing 116
   How Does The Lender Get Paid Back? 118
   Assigning The Tax Incentive 119
   Banking Restrictions 119

   19.   **Case Study** **121**
   Tax Rebate 121
   Tax Credit 124

   20.   **The Risks Of Cash-Flowing A Tax Incentive** .. **128**

   21.   **Will The Tax Incentive Jurisdiction Do What It Says It Will Do?** **130**
   Lower-Risk Counterparties 130
   So... There's No Risk? 131
   Slow Payment 132
   The Jurisdiction Runs Out Of Money 132
   Or Is Under-Funded 132
   A Change In The Tax Incentive Program 134
   Recapture 134
   Newer Programs 135

   22.   **Will You Do What You Say You Will Do?** **137**

Production Schedule 137
Filing The Books Correctly 139
Underspend.. 139
Unfinished Production...141

23. Completion Bond 144
What Is A Completion Bond? 144
Who Can Issue A Completion Bond?........................... 145
How Much Does A Completion Bond Cost................. 146
And Is It Worth It?.. 146
Alternatives To A Completion Bond............................ 148

PART FOUR 150

24. Shooting In A Location That Does Not Have A Tax Incentive.. 151
Weighing Up The Costs Versus The Benefits 151
Production Costs 152
Local Infrastructure And Favors 153
Specific Location 154
Travel Costs 155
Securing The Talent 156

25. Other Potential Benefits Of A Location 158
Costs And Attitude 159
Benefits For Writers And Directors.............................. 159
Grants 160
Subsidies 161
Studios As Investors.. 162
Location Scouting 163
Investment Vehicles... 163
International Co-Productions....................................... 166

26. The Final Word 168

AUTHOR'S NOTE 169

FURTHER INFORMATION 170
Other Books In This Series 170

ABOUT THE AUTHOR..171

PART ONE

1. What Is A Tax Incentive?

Many places in the world are looking for your business.

Whatever kind of business you are involved in, it will need to be based somewhere. But where? There are so many potential locations to choose from.

The race to win your business has become highly competitive. Location after location will try their best to persuade you to set up shop there.

One of the ways in which these places can entice you is by offering some kind of incentive to do business there rather than somewhere else.

This is how tax incentives first came to be.

Tax incentives are present in many industries across the world, be it property development, biotechnology or internet start-ups, to name just a few. Any time a country, state, city or region sees an opportunity to expand its growth, it will look to attract big businesses and infrastructure to base themselves there.

This is also true of the entertainment industry. The production of films and TV shows is big business, often with millions (or even hundreds of millions) of dollars being poured into a single production.

Countries, states, cities and regions across the world have seen the huge economic boost that can come from attracting big productions to shoot there. Their entire area can enjoy the benefits of production companies pouring large amounts of money into local employees, hotels, restaurants, stores, service providers, and lots of other local businesses.

And now, they want you!

As all these places compete to get your business, filmmakers are presented with opportunities like never before to choose the best place to shoot their content, both creatively and financially.

With just a little research, you can take advantage of these new opportunities to increase your chances of a successful and financially sound production.

In this book, we will explore:

- How you can use these tax incentives to your advantage

- How to balance the creative and financial needs of your production when choosing your shooting location

- How you can use tax incentives to help fund your production

- And much more...

Let's get started!

2. The Aims Of This Book

A lot of people ask: "Where is the best place to shoot a film or TV show?"

If only it were that simple...

If there were one place that was clearly 'The Best Place to Shoot', then everybody would be shooting there and you would already know about it, and this book wouldn't be necessary.

But there isn't. And that's a good thing. It keeps the market competitive and it keeps all the different jurisdictions working hard to attract your business.

No two productions are ever the same. No two finance plans are ever the same. And no two tax incentive programs work in exactly the same way.

Each one has different nuances and idiosyncrasies that provide both benefits and challenges. And one will likely suit the needs of your next production and your next investor better than your last one or the following one, depending on how you set them up.

The aim of this book is therefore not to provide a quick-fix solution to the challenge of choosing where to base your next production.

Rather, its aim is to walk you through the basic principles of how tax incentive programs work, both in the US and internationally, and arm you with all the knowledge you need to make an informed decision when choosing the perfect place to shoot your next film or TV show.

Who Is This Book For?

This book is aimed primarily at filmmakers and producers who are looking to get their film or TV show financed but need some help navigating some of the business fundamentals of the industry.

It is also aimed at financiers who might be new to the industry and want to understand how they can invest responsibly and then have the best chance of recouping their money.

Hollywood can be a tough place. People are rarely willing to sit down and explain this stuff to you. This book should make that minefield a lot more navigable.

Whether you're a producer, a writer or a director, a crew member, or a financier, grasping the importance of a production's location is crucial to understanding how it might get financed and produced.

Even if you're 'just' a creative person, long gone are the days when you could simply rely on other people to handle the business side for you.

In the independent world especially, everyone needs to have a basic understanding of how productions are financed to shape their projects in the right way and make themselves as valuable as possible. Only then will you be able to take control of your own destiny and drive a project to get made rather than waiting around for other people to tell you what to do.

Not An Incentives Guide

This book is not designed to be a guide to all the latest tax incentives in the US and around the world. My intention isn't to tell you what the incentive is in Louisiana and what it is in the Czech Republic.

Why?

Well, any such guide would likely be obsolete within a few months of it being published. The world of tax incentives changes constantly, and there's always a new tax incentive program or an improvement to an existing one that will come to the fore and be vying for your attention.

There are plenty of resources online where you can find indexes of these production incentives that are constantly being updated.

You can simply conduct a search for tax incentives, or visit the website of any film commission, and you will quickly find all the basic information you need about the specific tax incentive program you are searching for.

These tax incentives are constantly changing but the principles stay the same.

After reading this book, you will have the tools to look at these indexes, or other resources such as film commission websites, and understand what they are talking about, what is important to look for in each one and, most importantly, how they can actually help you to get your film or TV show financed and into production.

The world of tax incentives and locations can be a scary place, but having a basic understanding of it could make the difference between your next production being financed or not.

By the end of this book, you will have a much better grasp of:

- What tax incentives are

- How tax incentive programs work

- The different types of tax incentives that exist and how that might affect your bottom line

- What you need to consider when choosing the right location

- The questions you need to ask

- How to use a tax incentive to get financing up-front for your production

- What you should be looking for when choosing a location

- And much more...

3. An Overview Of Tax Incentives

In years gone by, the vast majority of film and TV production took place in a few select locations, which became known as 'production hubs'.

Production Hubs

Of all the production hubs in the world, the most recognizable is Los Angeles.

As the entertainment industry grew, it found a natural home in the southern California sunshine, and LA became the place where all the big stars and talent lived, relaxing in their glamorous homes in the Hollywood Hills or Bel Air.

A lot of talented crew followed them and made LA their home too. People set up studios there. An infrastructure was established, with equipment stores springing up and cameras and microphones and everything else you could imagine being built there.

In short, it became the place to make movies, and a system was established and everyone was happy.

Other production hubs sprang up across the world, particularly in large, fashionable, cosmopolitan cities such as New York, London, Paris and Rome, among many others. All the most diverse, modern and trendy places where production could take place easily and conveniently, which would be an attractive home to talent, and where crews could settle and work steadily.

Trouble is, whenever you have a monopoly in any field, prices go up and people become complacent about there being only one way to do things.

For people at the lower (or cheaper) end of the market, getting the services you need at the prices you can afford becomes tough. You're left looking for a new way of doing things.

That's a bit like what happened in the production world as people started looking for some other options.

'Non-Traditional' Shooting Locations

A few years ago, as the volume of independent production started to increase, other 'non-traditional' shooting locations began to spring up as an alternative to the traditional production hubs.

Suddenly, less well-known countries, states, cities and regions realized that they could provide a great product: new and interesting locations that hadn't been seen before, local talent, new studios, and much more, and all at a price that could be interesting to filmmakers and producers.

However, these new locations were faced with a problem: how do you persuade people to come and shoot in a place they are not familiar with? Where there might not be a lot of local crew or talent? Where you might have to pay additional money to fly people out there? To put them up in hotels? To pay them per diems (the daily allowance for crew members who are away from home) and feed them?

The answer: you offer them an incentive.

This incentive might offset any additional costs of locating your production there, and possibly much more, while they treat you like royalty and make you feel wanted.

On the back of these initiatives, over the last couple of decades, we have seen incredible growth in the production activity of 'non-traditional' shooting destinations such as Canada, Hungary, and the Czech Republic, as well as US states including Louisiana, Michigan and New Mexico, to name just a handful.

Consider All Options

Now, Los Angeles, New York, London and the rest are still wonderful places to make films and TV shows, as we will discuss later. In fact, many of these so-called production hubs now offer tax incentives as well, partially in a bid to counter these so-called 'runaway productions' that had been migrating elsewhere.

There are many benefits to shooting in these hubs, whatever your budget, and they should always be considered as possible locations.

However, if you haven't at least explored other options where a tax incentive might be available and can form part of your finance plan, then you might be leaving money on the table.

And nobody likes to do that...

4. How Does A Tax Incentive Work?

Before we get into the nitty gritty details, let's have a brief look at how tax incentives work in general terms.

Example

Let's say you go to shoot a film in North Carolina. At the time of writing, they offer a 25% tax rebate on qualifying expenditures (these are the expenses that can actually qualify for the incentive program – more on that shortly).

If that sounds complicated, don't worry! All will be explained.

But for now, let's say that you are spending $10m of qualified expenditures in North Carolina. A 25% tax rebate would be equal to $2.5m.

Once all your North Carolina production activities have been completed, and providing you have complied with all the necessary rules, you will get a tax rebate check back for $2.5m.

Of course, there are a few steps involved in that process, as we will cover shortly. **But overall, that's $2.5m you can give straight back to your investors.**

Getting 25% of your in-state spend back is a great way to start getting your financiers repaid before the film has even been distributed.

Using The Incentive To Raise Production Financing

For a lot of independent films, that $2.5m tax rebate is great, but they cannot afford to wait until production has been completed to take advantage of this cash. They might actually need that money up-front to help fund the production rather than just waiting to receive the tax incentive at the end.

Well, that's not a problem anymore. A lot of financiers have come up with structures to cash-flow these tax incentives before production starts. **This means that a producer can use the tax incentive to raise cash and then use this funding for the production itself, rather than wait until the end of the process to see any benefits.**

We'll go into this in much more detail later in the book.

A Sophisticated Landscape

Whilst a few years ago this was unfamiliar territory for many people, we now have a very sophisticated tax incentive landscape where practically every production – from small indie movies to studio blockbusters – is looking for the best deal.

Do some research online and you'll soon see that many of your favorite films and TV shows of the last few years have been shot in locations that you would never have guessed, far from the movie studios of Los Angeles or the mean streets of New York, even if that is what they look like.

All these productions, as well as thousands more, have had producers making decisions on which location best suited their project both creatively <u>and</u> financially.

You <u>can</u> have both.

These non-traditional locations would all have had a great combination of strong incentives, terrific landscapes and studio space, as well as excellent local crew, to become the perfect setting for each production.

As we move through this book, you will understand some of the decisions that the producers of these films and TV shows had to make in order to choose the right location for their productions, and how you can apply the same principles to yours.

5. Do I Need to Know Anything About Tax?

No.

Well, mostly... Let's put it this way: if you're producing a film or TV show, or running any kind of business, you need to have a basic understanding of taxes and how they work.

If you have that understanding down, and you have a capable accountant, there shouldn't be any issues in dealing with a tax incentive that should scare or worry you.

Stimulating The Economy

The 'tax' part of 'tax incentives' is important though. These incentives are often written into a jurisdiction's tax code and, in some (but not all) locations, the amount of the tax incentive might correlate with the local tax rates.

This money that is being handed to you isn't just being pulled out of the sky. It comes from public funds, which generally means that it's coming from the taxes paid by ordinary people and businesses in that location.

And in some cases, these tax incentives, particularly tax credits, are designed to be rolled straight back into the public funding system.

The idea behind tax incentives is that they are good for the local economy.

So, it's worth it for a region to offer a tax incentive to get your production there because that means that local residents are being hired, hotel rooms are being booked, restaurants are filling up, and rental equipment is being paid for.

The more income these local residents and businesses receive, the more tax dollars they will pay on that income, and so the money flows back into the tax system whilst also boosting the local economy and keeping residents employed and happy.

Because of this, tax incentives are governed and regulated by public bodies. This also means that the programs are voted on by the local legislature and usually come up for renewal on a regular basis.

If there is a shift in power or economic policy in that jurisdiction, or if it is felt that the tax incentive is not stimulating the economy sufficiently, they may vote to decrease the incentive amount or even scrap the program altogether.

Conversely, some jurisdictions may see the benefits enjoyed by a neighboring state or country from their tax incentive program and decide to introduce a brand new one to their region.

This is why it is essential to keep a close eye on a program's status before you commit to your shooting location, and why programs around the world are frequently changing.

Local Procedures

Due to the government-sponsored nature of tax incentives, you will have to go through certain procedures before they sign off on your credit or rebate. While this process may seem laborious, it is because of the responsibilities of handling public tax money that these checks and balances are in place.

In many jurisdictions, you will be subject to an audit before your tax incentive can be issued. You may also be required to file tax returns locally for the SPV (the 'special purpose vehicle', which is the company you will likely have to set up specifically to produce that film or TV show).

The local authorities will want to see evidence that you have spent what you say you have spent there. They can then do their own calculations of your qualifying spend to work out exactly what your tax incentive amount should be.

Having a good production accountant, and possibly a lawyer that can advise you on the local legislation, means that this process shouldn't be a problem for most producers.

Transparency

Why is all this important?

When dealing with these organizations, transparency is key. These are not private financiers who may be able to bend the rules, jump outside their model, or make an exception for you on this one occasion. They will not be able to include additional expenses that aren't written into their program. They must follow the procedures as required by their local legislation and tax code.

But you have an A-list star? Doesn't matter. But have they seen what you're doing for their region? Doesn't matter. But do they know who your father is? Does. Not. Matter.

These local agencies are answerable to the public. This is, after all, public tax money that they are using and that you're trying to get. **You have to justify it to them so that they can justify it to the taxpayers.**

Stick To The Rules

If anybody tells you that they can sneak a little extra in as qualifying spend, ignore them. The regulations for these incentives are usually legally-binding bills that have been drafted by local governing bodies and you need to be respectful of that. There really shouldn't be any wiggle-room or flexibility within those laws.

That's not to say there aren't things that you can and should do to maximize your qualifying spend, as we will discuss.

But remember, you pay taxes too. How would you feel if a producer came to wherever you live and took more public funding than they were actually entitled to? What if you discovered that your tax money was being diverted from schools and hospitals and instead being handed over to a producer that had just been 'bending the rules' a little to get more funding for their production?

You likely wouldn't be pleased about that. It happens rarely but, when it does happen, it's regarded quite seriously.

As long as you stick to the rules, you should be fine.

Following the guidelines closely and working with the right people in the local authorities means you should have a great experience in whichever location you choose, and hopefully you'll go back there again in the future!

6. Choosing Your Location

There are a variety of tax incentives in any number of locations around the world and they are all different.

The possibilities this presents are really exciting but all of this information can also seem a little overwhelming.

Where do you start? Who is offering what? And how do you begin to narrow down some of your choices?

Start With The Creative

The first place to start is with the creative aspects of your script. Think of locations that would serve your story creatively, regardless of the tax incentive.

For all our talk of financials and budgets, this is <u>still</u> the most important question for you to ask. If the landscape, the environment, or even the local population don't match what's in the script, then a certain location might be wrong for you, however fantastic their incentive program may be.

If a location is not an organic fit for you creatively, you either need to re-work the script, or you need to find a different location. Otherwise, you're trying to fit a square peg into a round hole and your project may suffer as a result.

Sometimes, it just doesn't work, no matter how hard you try.

If your story is mainly interiors and can be done on a sound stage anywhere in the world, then that's great. Your pool of potential locations is almost endless.

However, if your story is set in the sweltering hot jungle, then shooting somewhere in northern Canada probably isn't going to be the right fit for you, even if their tax incentive were the best in the world.

And if your story is set on the streets of a big American city, then shooting in a remote location in Eastern Europe might not work for you either, even if they are offering a better tax incentive than somewhere closer to home.

It's always worth looking at comparable productions and seeing where they were shot. Although they might have had a very specific reason for choosing their location, the producers may already have done a lot of the research and cost comparisons for you.

Speak to as many people in the industry as possible and see where they have shot recently and where they have had good or bad experiences.

How Do I Find Out About A Location's Tax Incentive?

Once you have a few ideas, the best place to find out about any tax incentive program is by contacting the local film office or film commission representing that location.

You should start by checking their website, where most of the details you need to know will already be listed.

Pretty much every established location these days has a website outlining the main elements of their tax incentive program. If there are any gaps that you need filling in, just pick up the phone and call them, or drop them an e-mail.

They want your business and you'll usually find them quite eager to respond and help you through the process.

Ask them as many questions as you think might be helpful. There are no 'stupid questions' in this business, and if they really want to attract your production to their area, their film commissioner should be willing to work with you as much as possible.

There are also various independent companies that create their own compendium of all the different tax incentive programs across the world, almost like a comparison guide. This should usually be available online or as a pamphlet that you can order, and can be a really useful guide in giving you an overview of each program, sometimes directly comparing them side-by-side.

Starting the process is as easy as getting on your computer, performing a search for production incentives, and away you go!

Everybody is looking to attract you to their location which, as mentioned earlier, makes it a very competitive playing field as these locations try their best to woo you and stop you from going to their competitors.

The people working at these local film offices should be courteous and helpful. Ask them whatever you want, they've probably heard it all before, and they should be able to lay out clearly the benefits that they offer and how large a tax incentive they can realistically provide.

Remember though: these numbers only tell half the story, as we shall see shortly.

7. How Much Money Will A Tax Incentive Generate?

This is the question that everyone wants answered!

To understand how much money you will get back from a tax incentive, it is vitally important to understand the rules of the program in your shooting location.

Remember, every location and program is different, so don't assume that the numbers will be the same wherever you go.

The Incentive As A Percentage

Most locations will express their tax incentive as a percentage. A typical headline for a tax incentive program might look like this:

"20% tax rebate on all qualifying spend"

But what does this mean?

We'll go into this in more detail shortly but here's the most important thing:

This does not automatically mean you will get 20% of your entire budget back!

You might find producers who just assume that the tax incentive will cover 20% of their budget. But that most likely wouldn't be correct. That percentage rarely covers the full amount of a budget.

The key is in the term 'qualifying spend'.

Before you can even estimate how much the tax incentive will eventually be worth, you will need to see which items in your budget can be included in your final tax incentive amount, and which cannot.

So, while these large numbers might sound great as a headline, what do they actually mean in practical terms, and how much money will they ultimately generate for you?

Let's take a look...

8. Qualifying Spend

In order to understand how tax incentives work, you must understand the concept of qualifying spend. This is the key term to look out for when combing through any local legislation on tax incentives.

It may also be referred to as:

- Qualifying expenditures

- Qualifying expenses

- Qualifying costs

- Or any other similar term...

What Is Qualifying Spend?

In most cases, tax incentives do not work simply as a percentage of your overall budget.

Instead, you need to look at each individual line item or expenditure in your budget and see whether that item qualifies under the terms of the tax incentive program you are applying for.

Only certain items will qualify for each program, and this changes everywhere you go.

Wherever you are, you need to separate what does qualify from what doesn't qualify in order to determine what your qualifying spend will be. The tax incentive that you generate will be a percentage of that qualifying spend only.

If there is a line item in your budget that is not part of the qualifying spend, then that item will not count towards your tax incentive.

Which Items Can Be Included As Qualifying Spend?

The items that qualify for a tax incentive can change from state to state, region to region, country to country.

No two tax incentive programs are ever the same, so you need to determine which expenses will qualify and which expenses will not qualify in the particular location you are interested in shooting in.

For example, you might find a program in the US that <u>does</u> allow you to claim the tax incentive on the salaries paid to local crew members that are residents of the state in which you are shooting. However, it may <u>not</u> allow you to claim for the salaries paid to any out-of-state crew members that are hired.

In this case, only the salaries of local resident hires would count as qualifying spend. You would not get any money back for the salaries of non-resident hires that travel to your location just for the production and then leave.

Even though the salaries of out-of-state hires might not count, you may still be allowed to claim the tax incentive on the hotel rooms you put them up in, as well as per diems, meals and other expenses, all depending on the local legislation.

The same program might allow you to claim a tax incentive on any equipment that you buy locally in their state. However, it might <u>not</u> allow you to claim on the shipping of any equipment that you bring in from out-of-state.

These are examples of just some of the possible regulations that you will need to learn about.

So, you need to read the legislation very carefully and consider every single line item in your budget to see which expenditures might qualify, however large or small.

Analyzing The Legislation

An easier way to illustrate this is to make a chart of all the major items that will and will not qualify for the tax incentive in your chosen location.

For example:

QUALIFYING SPEND	NON-QUALIFYING SPEND
Below-the-Line Salaries for Residents	Below-the-Line Salaries for Non-Residents
Hotel Rooms	Above-the-Line Salaries
Equipment Rentals (if made in-state)	Financing Fees
Travel Expenses (if booked through a local agent)	Development Expenses
Payroll Fees (if using a local company)	Equipment Transportation Costs

In this case, all the items that are in the first column under 'Qualifying Spend' can be included in your final tax incentive calculations. You will get a percentage back of all of these expenses.

Those that are in the second column under 'Non-Qualifying Spend' cannot be included in your final tax incentive calculations. You will not get anything back for any of these expenses.

So, let's go back to our previous example of a location's incentive of 20% of all qualifying spend.

Applying this to our chart, this means that you could claim back 20% of the amount spent in that location on the following items:

- Salaries of below-the-line crew members if they are residents of that location

- Costs of all hotel rooms in that location

- Costs of any equipment rentals from vendors in that location

- Costs of any travel expenses booked through a vendor in that location

- Any payroll fees if using a company based in that location

However, you cannot claim anything for the following expenses:

- Salaries of below-the-line crew members that are not residents of that location

- Salaries of any above-the-line crew members (including principal cast), whether or not they are residents of that location

- Any financing fees

- Any expenses associated with the project's development

- Costs incurred in the transportation of equipment

Different Ways Of Comparing This Information

Alternatively, we could express this information in another way:

ITEM	QUALIFYING SPEND
Below-the-Line Salaries for Residents	YES
Below-the-Line Salaries for Non-Residents	NO
Above-the-Line Salaries	NO
Hotel Rooms	YES
Equipment Rentals (if made in-state)	YES
Financing Fees	NO
Development Expenses	NO
Travel Expenses (if booked through a local agent)	YES
Payroll Fees (if using a local company)	YES
Equipment Transportation Costs	NO

When you are first choosing and comparing tax incentives, forming a table or chart like the ones here can be a really useful visual aid when deciding what is best for your production.

Once you get into more detail, you will look to break this down even further by each line item. This will also help when comparing locations.

In those cases, you may create a spreadsheet to compare what does and doesn't count as qualifying spend in each location.

Let's say you are comparing the qualifying items in three different locations. Your spreadsheet might look something like this:

ITEM	LOCATION A (40%)	LOCATION B (35%)	LOCATION C (25%)
Director	No	Yes	Yes
Actors	No	No	Yes
Gaffer	Yes	Yes	Yes
Grip	Yes	Yes	Yes
Hotels	Yes	No	Yes
Camera Rental	Yes	No	Yes

This is another helpful way to compare and contrast each tax incentive and its qualifying spend allowances in relation to your budget.

You can clearly see here that Location C offers a lower tax incentive rate than locations A and B, but their qualifying spend includes a lot more. So, as we will discuss shortly, Location A's higher number of 40% may not actually be the best option, depending on the amounts that you have budgeted for your director and actors.

9. Why Won't My Entire Budget Qualify For The Tax Incentive?

So, as we have seen, a 20% tax incentive almost never means that you will have 20% of your budget covered.

It is a mistake that many producers and filmmakers make. They see the headline number and don't consider some of the details and nuances of the production process.

You're probably not going to spend your entire budget in that location, particularly if it is not where you are usually based. And if you do, parts of it might not count as qualifying spend.

Aside from the qualifying spend restrictions during filming, there are other parts of the production process that you should take into account.

Some of the major budget items to consider here include:

Development

Development costs can sometimes be a grey area when it comes to tax incentives.

For our purposes, these mostly refer to costs in the optioning of the intellectual property and the nurturing of the script. They might also refer to some of your earliest infrastructural expenditures.

Development costs might therefore include:

- Story rights

- Book options

- Re-write fees

- Incorporation of your production company

- Legal fees associated with the above

- And much more...

In some instances, such expenditures can amount to significant costs in a budget – it would be nice to get a tax incentive on some of these!

Some jurisdictions, having been burnt by producers trying to take advantage of certain loopholes, simply do not allow any development costs to be included.

Others allow certain development costs to be included, but have proceeded with some caution and have very specific wording as to what can be claimed on and what cannot.

However, most development costs are commonly incurred at the very earliest stages of the production process. This can be long before a shooting location has even been considered, let alone locked in, and will probably be transacted in the filmmaker's home location.

For this reason, these development costs can rarely be included in a tax incentive calculation unless they were made in the eventual shooting location.

Other costs that are generally incurred later in the development process might be more acceptable.

For example, if you were to travel on a location scout, you might be able to include some or all of the expenses associated with that trip in your eventual tax incentive calculations if you end up shooting there.

However, you need to check very carefully which development costs, if any, can be included in your final calculations according to the specific legislation with which you are working.

Post-Production, VFX And Delivery Costs

As any producer knows, post-production can be a very long and costly process.

It can form a large portion of your entire budget, particularly if your film or TV show is visual effects-heavy or requires some special post services.

Most jurisdictions will allow you to include your post-production costs in their incentive program. While this is helpful, you have to consider the practical implementation of this.

Think back to the very opening of this book and our discussion about production hubs versus non-traditional locations. Most filmmakers end up being based in one production hub or another, and are not usually spread out across the country or based in non-traditional shooting locations.

This means that, when shooting in a non-traditional location, most of the significant creative crew members, including the producers, director, writer and editor, will not be permanently based there.

It isn't always easy to persuade a director or producer to leave their homes, families and daily obligations back in Los Angeles, London or New York to go to a non-traditional shooting location for two or three months or more to pre-produce and then shoot their film or TV show there.

While non-traditional locations can be a wonderful place to base your production, it places a strain on people to live out of hotel rooms and be separated from their families for long periods of time.

Most filmmakers are willing to make this sacrifice for the duration of pre-production and filming as they know that a production tax incentive can help greenlight their project.

However, asking them to do this for another four to six months for the duration of post-production as well can often be a step too far.

Most producers accept that a filmmaker will make this sacrifice for the duration of filming on the basis that they can then complete post-production back at home where they can sleep in their own bed and be with their family again.

This means that most post-production costs rarely get included in tax incentive calculations for non-traditional shooting locations.

Additionally, given that the post-production process can last many months, sometimes even longer, the cost of additional hotel rooms, meals, per diems and other expenses for your director, producers, editor and other team members might make this process prohibitively expensive, even if you can still get a tax incentive on all of these costs.

And of course, many of the best and most reliable post-production and VFX ('visual effects') houses, as well as the labs to produce deliverables, are based back in those production hubs such as Los Angeles, New York and London.

Even though there are some wonderful post-production facilities springing up all over the US and the rest of the world in non-traditional locations, the vast majority of this work takes place back in those production hubs.

For these reasons, many producers simply ignore their post-production, VFX and delivery costs when calculating their tax incentive, even if the legislation does allow for those expenditures to be included in the qualifying spend.

That being said, this situation is constantly evolving.
As I mentioned, there are some wonderful facilities springing up outside of these traditional production hubs and it would be foolish not to see how you could take advantage of them.

Many of these new studios have spent a lot of money investing in post-production facilities and have anticipated these potential issues. With some amazing new technology, some of this work can now be done remotely, where your director and producers might still be able to oversee the process from a studio in Los Angeles even while the actual editing work is taking place in a facility thousands of miles away.

This might still be included in the tax incentive if a local studio is being used and local residents are being hired.

Indeed, some jurisdictions have spotted a gap in the market and have created tax incentives specifically centered around industries such as VFX. They have invested in the latest studios and technology to attract filmmakers to that location which has become known for its incredible VFX work. For a project heavy in special effects, this could be significant.

So, when it comes to calculating the tax incentive, think of the practical implications of this.

Just because your post-production costs can be included, this doesn't mean that you will realistically spend all (or any) of them in your shooting location.

Be sure to ask what can be included from your post-production budget, remotely or otherwise, and see which work could actually be performed there.

ATL And BTL

One of the major items that producers look for is whether their above-the-line (also known as 'ATL') expenditures will qualify.

Above-the-line generally encompasses the salaries for cast and crew members regarded as the creative elements of the film or TV show. What is considered to be above-the-line can vary from place to place so read the guidelines of your tax incentive program carefully.

If above-the-line expenses can be included, this could make a huge difference to the final value of your incentive. It means you could include the salaries and certain other expenses of:

- The director

- The writer

- The actors

- The producers

Some places have different definitions of what counts as above-the-line. So, in certain cases, this may also include the salaries of the HOD's ('Heads of Department') and other crew members, including:

- The casting director

- The director of photography

- The editor

- And certain others...

As there may be some discrepancy between locations as to what counts as above-the-line and what doesn't, many film commissions will have a breakdown for every single cast and crew position and whether they qualify for their tax incentive or not.

They can tell you very quickly and easily whether they consider someone above-the-line or not. When in doubt, just ask them!

In contrast, most tax incentive programs will allow you to include the salaries of your below-the-line ('BTL') crew members.

This generally encompasses anyone outside your core creative team and includes the vast majority of the crew (whether the gaffer, the grip, the set decorator, the props person and so on), many of whom will be paid standard union rates set on a daily or weekly basis.

You may still have to note whether these below-the-line crew members are local residents or non-residents, as we will discuss shortly.

As the above-the-line individuals often get paid the highest salaries, it is crucial to know whether or not these expenses can be included in your qualifying spend for the tax incentive program you are going for.

Think about it like this: if you have a big star that is being paid $1m, that's a significant amount of money. It would be worth a lot if you were to receive some kind of tax incentive for that amount.

Let's apply this to our example at the end of the last chapter. You could go to a location that has a 40% tax incentive program but does not include above-the-line expenses. In that case, that $1m salary for your big star would not qualify. So, you would get nothing back for that but you would get 40% back on all the below-the-line salaries for your crew.

Or you could go to a location that has a 25% program but which does include above-the-line expenses. In that case, you can get 25% back for that $1m salary, which is a lot of money. But you would also only get 25% back for the rest of the salaries too, rather than 40% as in our first example.

Which option is better? That depends on the rest of your budget and the unique structure of your production.

If you have a huge shoot with hundreds of below-the-line crew members, you may be better off selecting the first location where you can get 40% back on all their salaries, even though you would get nothing back for the $1m salary of your star.

Conversely, if your crew is rather small and their salaries are less significant than in the first example, you may prefer to take an incentive of 25% of their salaries which, coupled with 25% of the star's $1m salary, will represent a better deal for you financially.

Ultimately, it comes down to simple math as to what makes sense for your production, as we will see a little later.

Resident Labor And Non-Resident Labor

As mentioned earlier, most tax incentive programs were started for a location to boost its local economy.

This means that, ideally, they will want to see as many local residents as possible being employed.

When choosing a location, look at its tax incentive program and see whether it differentiates between:

- Local resident labor

    o Usually someone with a driver's license or permanent residence there that pays local taxes

- Non-resident labor

    o Someone that is not based in that location and must be brought in from somewhere else specifically for the production

Some locations will <u>not</u> allow you to include the salaries or certain expenses of anyone that is not a local resident in their tax incentive program. In that case, for anyone that you bring in from another location, you will get <u>nothing</u> back for them.

Other locations <u>will</u> allow you to include some or all non-residents. However, some will offer an additional tax incentive for the use of local resident labor as opposed to non-resident labor as governing bodies want to encourage and incentivize you to hire locally as much as possible.

Even then, you need to clarify whether above-the-line salaries will qualify for your tax incentive, whether for local residents or otherwise. If actors' salaries cannot be included in the qualifying spend, then it won't matter whether an actor is a local resident or not.

So, you could find a situation where, even if a member of your above-the-line team is a resident of that location, they will not count towards the incentive.

Conversely, in a different location, you might find that a member of your above-the-line team that is not a resident will count towards that incentive. It just depends on the local legislation.

If non-residents can be included as qualifying spend, there may still be some requirements as to how they are paid (for example, through a local loan-out company) or how they file taxes for that income.

However great the incentive may be to hire local residents, you will still need to research a location's production scene thoroughly to take advantage of it. If there is an incentive for hiring local resident labor, be sure to verify whether there is actually enough local crew to fill the positions that you might need.

It's all very well for a location to offer you an additional incentive to employ local crew, but if there is none available then it's not going to help you much. And if there are crew members available, are they of a high enough standard to match your expectations?

In places where the local crew base is not very deep, try to get a sense of what else is shooting there at the same time as you.

Are you a small independent movie competing with a large network TV series for the same crew? If so, you might find high-quality local resident labor to be scarce. You would then need to bring in crew members from somewhere else, which not only incurs an additional cost but also may not even qualify for the tax incentive.

So, a little bit of research in this area can make a big impact when choosing your shooting location and incentive program.

10. Calculating The Tax Incentive Value

Once you have established what counts as qualifying spend, it's time to work with your line producer and go through the budget in detail, line by line, to establish exactly what will qualify and what will not, and how much each item will likely be worth in your tax incentive calculations.

As you go through the budget, you can make a note next to each line item as to how much that will generate from the tax incentive program in your chosen shooting location.

The easiest way to do this is to make a replica of your current budget and add a couple of columns.

Example

As an example, and to keep it very simple, let's consider a location with an overall tax incentive that comprises the following:

- 20% on all qualifying expenditures

- All BTL labor included (both local and non-resident)

- Additional 10% for any local resident BTL labor (giving a total of 30% on those salaries)

- All non-crew-related in-state expenditures included (equipment, hotels, meals etc.)
- No ATL labor included

- No out-of-state expenses of any sort included

So, you would take this information and apply it carefully to your budget, noting (or at least making an informed assumption) which of your crew members will be local and will thereby qualify for the additional 10%.

You would then add two extra columns at the end (or create a separate table, as we've done here) to show the likely benefits of each item from your tax incentive expressed as both a percentage and as a dollar amount:

DESCRIPTION	TOTAL	INCENTIVE (%)	INCENTIVE ($)
Director	50,000	X	0
Actor	80,000	X	0
Art Director	17,500	20%	3,500
Gaffer	12,250	30%	3,675
Sound Kit	7,000	20%	1,400
TOTAL:	**166,750**		**8,575**

Again, this table is designed to be just an excerpt from your budget and not indicative of the actual prices you should be paying anyone.

But when you take your budget and break it down in this way, you'll quickly have a really clear idea of how much the tax incentive should eventually generate.

There is even budgeting software out there that can do this for you, allowing you to tag qualifying items into specific groups. You could use this to calculate the likely tax incentive for you.

Assumptions

As accurate as your budget might be, you will probably have to make some assumptions along the way.

For example, early in the budgeting process, you will have to make an assumption as to how many crew members will be local residents or otherwise. Given that you are only likely to start crewing up once pre-production starts, it is hard to predict this with total accuracy while you are still putting your financing together.

But, as you get closer to your start date, you should be able to make a really informed and close estimate of what the final numbers should be.

Again, this will be based partly on your knowledge of the local production scene and its crew base, as well as your research into what else is shooting there at the same time and may be competing for the same crew members.

The local film commission should be happy to work with you to help you identify and utilize all its local crew and resources.

There are also a number of independent companies who can be hired to do this analysis for you for a fee and even make suggestions as to how you can maximize your tax incentive returns.

11. Maximizing The Value Of Your Tax Incentive

You must be extremely careful to comply with all local legislation and work with the film commission to ensure that there is absolutely no fraudulent behavior when claiming the tax incentive.

However, you should also work with the film commission and your line producer to ensure that you are not missing out on certain expenses that, with a bit of effort and creativity, could legally and legitimately be included in your qualifying spend and increase your tax incentive amount.

Some examples include the following:

- Check to see whether an in-state vendor might be able to do the same job as the out-of-state vendor you were going to use. If they can, and they can match any discounts your usual vendor offers you, you should check whether those expenses can now qualify for your tax incentive

    o For example, can you use a local travel agent to book all the travel for your production? If so, perhaps those travel expenses will now qualify whereas they wouldn't if they were booked with an external travel agent

- When choosing your payroll company, ask whether they have a local office in the location where you are looking to shoot. If they do, their fees may also qualify for the tax incentive

- In some jurisdictions, you can set up a local loan-out or pay-through company to pay salaries during your production (and in some places, this is a requirement). The expense of this might then also be included

- You will find some locations that might include certain budgeted fees in their tax incentive program, such as executive producer fees or financing fees. Be aware of what qualifies and what doesn't, and then see whether there is any flexibility in assigning the roles on your crew or setting up your production financing

    - For example, perhaps you have a major US bank providing a production loan. If they have a local branch in the state where you are shooting, they might be able to conduct the transaction through that branch and then the finance fees can qualify as local spend

There are many other examples of this and you should always seek guidance wherever possible to make sure you are maximizing your tax incentive and <u>not</u> leaving any money on the table.

Ask around and find other producers and filmmakers who have used the system before and see what they did (or what they wished they had done!) in order to maximize the incentive.

Again though, I must stress, do not try to beat or cheat the system. All of these suggestions only work if they are legal and fully disclosed, in close collaboration with the local film commission.

If you try to work outside their very strict parameters, you could get into a lot of trouble. But stay within their guidelines and you should have a good experience.

PART TWO

12. What Kinds of Tax Incentives Are There?

There are various kinds of tax incentives that exist across the world. Each one works in a slightly different way.

These can vary greatly from location to location but, by and large, the principles remain the same.

For ease of use, in this book we are going to focus on the US state tax incentives for our examples and templates.

However, you can apply the theories that we are discussing here to practically any jurisdiction in the world with just a little research on how that program works.

In the US, there are two main forms of state-based tax incentives:

- Tax rebates

    o These are cash rebates that are offered back to you once production is completed

    o You would get a check for the appropriate amount, which makes things nice and simple

- Tax credits

    o These are certificates of credit that can be applied against your (or someone else's) local taxes in the jurisdiction that you shot in

A couple of states do have variations or versions of these, such as tax refunds, which have a similar principle but require a little more detail.

However, the two listed here are by far the most common types of tax incentive that you will come across, both in the US and internationally.

The principles applied to these incentives can be replicated for just about any other kind of production tax incentive you will come across.

Let's take a look at these in more detail...

13. Tax Rebates

Let's deal with tax rebates first.

They're the ones that everyone wants. Most of the time, they are simpler, less work, more money, and altogether less 'tax-y', which is good.

I've chosen to start with tax rebates because most people already know what a rebate is. **You spend some cash, and then you get some cash back, usually a portion or percentage of the original amount spent.**

This is a good place to begin as it involves fewer steps than tax credits.

Basic Principles

We already discussed the basic principles a little earlier: once you have finished production in your chosen location, you then go through all the necessary procedures to turn over your books, receipts and numbers to the local authorities to verify your qualifying spend.

In many places, those local authorities will want to do an audit on your books and check that you have actually spent what you say you have.

Whether your budget is $100,000 or $100,000,000, it is really important to keep accurate books, receipts, invoices, and anything else that might support your numbers relating to local spend.

As always, make sure you are in compliance with any other regulations they have, some examples of which we discuss later in this book.

Be thorough, and work with the film commission to make sure you've not forgotten anything.

Once everything is checked and approved, and they are satisfied with the expenses you have made, they will issue you a rebate check.

This will be for a percentage of your qualifying spend according to their local legislation, as per our example earlier.

In that case, we had an incentive program offering a tax rebate of 20% of our qualifying spend.

Let's assume our qualifying spend equaled $1m. Then, the rebate check would be for $200k.
If the qualifying spend were $10m, then the rebate check would be for $2m.

And so on...

You can then bank that check and, most likely, you will use it to start paying back your investors, or to cover any outstanding debts you might have. If the rebate is generated quickly enough and the local legislation allows for it, you may even be able to use this for your post-production costs, although many jurisdictions will take a good few months to process your check or want to see a finished product before issuing the rebate so you shouldn't count on this.

Case Study

Let's imagine we have a film with a $10m budget that we are shooting in a US state with a tax rebate.

Let's assume for this example that the general overview of the program is as follows:

- 20% tax rebate for all qualifying expenses that are made in-state

- Includes both BTL and ATL expenditures

- Includes both resident and non-resident labor

- Does <u>not</u> include any development costs or expenditures made out-of-state

- Additional 10% for any local residents that are hired (so a total of 30% of their salaries)

So, we have gone through our budget line-by-line and noted which expenses qualify and which do not.

Remember, we are only calculating the tax rebate on the qualifying spend and <u>not</u> on the total budget.

Assuming all our development, post-production, special effects and delivery costs were made out-of-state at a total cost of $3m, this is a significant difference.

We now know what our tax rebate will finally be worth, as follows:

BUDGET:	$10,000,000		
In-State Qualifying Expenses (excluding Local Hires)	$4,000,000	Tax Rebate of 20%	$800,000
Local Hires	$3,000,000	Tax Rebate of 30%	$900,000
TOTAL:			**$1,700,000**

So, on this basis, we will generate a tax rebate of **$1,700,000**.

This is 17% of our $10m budget, which should make our investors very happy indeed!

They get to recoup a big chunk of their investment immediately without giving away any equity in the project. Everyone wins!

Once we have submitted our receipts and expenses to the local authorities, it is just a question of waiting for them to process everything and, if everything is in order, send us a check.

These numbers are just an example but they are realistic depending on the type of movie that we might be shooting.

If, for example, we could do all our post-production and special effects in that state, that would increase our tax rebate numbers significantly.

Also, you may find a location that does allow you to include development costs and other expenditures that aren't included in this example, which again would increase these numbers.

It all just depends on the program and the specifics of the production itself.

14. Tax Credits

Tax credits work on the same principle we've already discussed: you spend some cash, you get some cash back.

And much of the process is very similar to the tax rebate we just went through, up until the point that the credit itself is issued.

And that's where it gets interesting...

Basic Principles

Rather than giving you a check that you can then take back home with you to Los Angeles or New York or wherever you live, some states prefer to keep that money within their tax system.

Usually, this makes their incentive program easier to justify to the general public.

Remember how I said that you have to bear in mind the 'tax' part of tax incentives? This is what I was talking about.

So, instead of getting a check from the local authorities, you get a certificate. The certificate will have a dollar amount that you can use when paying your taxes in that state.

A tax credit is <u>not</u> simply 'money in the bank' like a rebate check. It is designed to offset part or all of the taxes that you owe in that location.

So, when you are required to file a tax return in that state, you can use your tax credit certificate to reduce your tax bill by that amount.

How To Use A Tax Credit

Now, this is pretty straightforward if you are based in the state where you have a tax credit and have a large tax liability there.

Let's say your production company is based in Louisiana and it has to pay $3m in taxes. That's $3m in cash that you have to find from somewhere.

If you have a Louisiana tax credit certificate worth $1m, you can apply that amount against your $3m tax bill.

This will reduce your tax bill in Louisiana by $1m. This means that, instead of the original $3m you owed in taxes, you now owe only $2m. In other words, the tax credit certificate saves you $1m in cash.

We could lay this example out as follows:

Taxes You Owe		**$3,000,000**
	MINUS	
Tax Credit		$1,000,000
	EQUALS	
Amount of Taxes You Now Owe		**$2,000,000**

So, if you have a tax credit certificate in a state or region where you are already paying taxes, this can end up being just as good as having the cash in your pocket.

But What If I Don't Pay Taxes In That Location?

The challenge with tax credits is, particularly in non-traditional shooting locations, most production companies aren't based there, and nor are the individuals that are running them.

As we discussed earlier, most production companies will come to that state specifically to take advantage of their tax incentive program.

They would come in and form a new company, a special purpose vehicle. This SPV acts as the production company for that one production alone and is then shut down once all its business has been concluded.

In many states, the SPV won't have very much tax liability. It may not even have to file tax returns there at all.

If that's the case with your production, then that tax credit certificate isn't worth very much to you.

What Do I Do With My Tax Credit?

Even if the tax credit is not worth anything to you, it is worth something to someone else. Someone that has a large tax liability in that state.

Maybe it's a huge corporation that is headquartered there. Maybe it's a local multi-millionaire who has holdings, assets or income that are taxable at state level.

Whoever it is, they might owe millions of dollars in taxes at the end of the fiscal year.

They will also have accountants and advisers whose job it is to lessen the amount that they have to pay in taxes as much as possible. They will be looking for every way to get that tax bill lower.

And for every dollar they save, their bosses will think they are doing a great job.

These people will be out there looking for tax credits that they can use against their company's tax liability. Tax credits just like yours.

You have something that they want and they will be looking to buy it from you.

Selling A Tax Credit

You want to sell them your credit. And they want to buy it from you. It's a match made in heaven!

Except...

They don't want to buy it from you at full price.

To purchase any tax credit not only takes them extra time but also incurs additional costs for legal fees and tax analysis, as well as the process of negotiating with brokers and sellers.

So, they're not going to pay you $1m for a tax credit certificate that only reduces their taxes by $1m.

For the cost, time and effort of making that transaction, they would be better off just paying the $1m in taxes.

If you make it worth their while, they will still buy it from you. But they will only do so at a discount.

Let's say they offer to buy your tax credit certificate for 80 cents on the dollar, or, expressed another way, at 80% of its full value. This means they are buying $1m of tax credits for just $800,000.

Now they've saved $200,000. And that's when it becomes interesting for them...

Understanding Pricing

Once you've found someone to sell your tax credit to, you'll need to negotiate a price.

First, you need to understand the different ways of discussing the pricing of tax credit purchases.

People might refer to the pricing in several different ways. They usually all amount to the same thing.

Some of the most commons ones are:

- As a dollar amount

    o   In other words, our tax credit is worth $1m, and the buyer will purchase it for $800,000

- As a percentage

    o   In the same transaction, the buyer is purchasing the tax credit for 80% of its face value

- As 'cents on the dollar'

    o   In this transaction, the buyer is purchasing the tax credit for 80 cents on the dollar (or 80c/$). This means that, for every dollar of tax credit they are buying, they are paying 80 cents for it, regardless of what the final number is

Now that you understand how the pricing is expressed, it's time to get into the numbers.

How Much Is My Tax Credit Worth?

Great question. And the answer is: it depends.

When establishing the price for any product, it's all about 'supply and demand'. Tax credits are no different. When supply is low and demand is high, prices go up, and vice versa.

The pricing can change dramatically from location to location. What you could sell a tax credit for in one location is not an indicator of how much you could sell it for in another.

Many different factors determine how much you can sell your tax credit for, including:

- In some states, tax liability is particularly high, which increases the demand for tax credits and can drive prices up

- In certain places, there might be a lot of tax credits floating around (not just from film and TV production, but from other industries too) which can drive prices down as supply is high

- Some states have a lot of big corporations in them, which means that there should be a lot of demand for these credits as these huge companies will have a high tax liability...

- ...but maybe there are a lot of corporations in the state precisely because corporation tax is low – that can drive the price of tax credits down too

- The time of year is also important. If you have a tax credit to sell in the two months before people have to file their local taxes in that state, then you're in luck. People are worried about their taxes, they've done their calculations, they know the exact amount of their tax liability and they know what they need to reduce it. Demand is higher and so are prices

- However, if you wait until the beginning of the next fiscal year, you might find that there is less urgency to buy tax credits as people do not yet know what their tax liability is for that year and paying their taxes is not something they want to think about for a good few months yet. As you don't want to have this certificate on your hands for another ten months, you may have to sell it at a lower price as demand will be less when it is not 'tax season'

- And much more...

All of these are factors to consider when calculating the eventual benefit to your production from a tax credit certificate. This in turn will be important in deciding which location and tax incentives program you choose.

Tax Credit Brokers

This all sounds very complicated, right?

It certainly was for me the first time I had a tax credit that I needed to sell. I remember thinking: 'How on earth am I supposed to find a buyer for my tax credit in a place that's a thousand miles away and where I don't know anyone?'

Most people will look to a local broker to help them navigate this minefield.

As in other industries, the broker acts a middle man, sitting between the two parties to facilitate the transaction. For most producers, a broker is the best way to sell a tax credit.

As a producer, do you really have time to start calling every single corporation in a state you don't know and seeing who needs tax credits and how much they'll pay you for them? You probably have other things to be doing.

A local broker will already know the necessary people to contact and will likely have a database of clients already set up. The broker will know who is looking to buy tax credits and where, how much they need, and how much they are willing to spend.

Crucially, a broker should also be able to advise what the going rate is for you to sell your tax credit.

They should give you a fairly accurate representation of the price that they can get for you. As their job is commission-based, it's in their interests to get as high a price as possible for a seller.

Choosing A Broker

It's usually a good idea to speak to a few different brokers and make sure they are all giving you similar information.

After all, one broker may claim they can get you a higher price than another, so it pays to shop around.

For example, one broker in a certain state might claim they have a client who will buy $1m of tax credits for 80 cents on the dollar (80c/$).

You may find another who claims they can get you 82c/$ but only needs $500,000 of tax credits for their client.

Another may have a client who will only pay 78c/$ but will take as much as you can give them.

Shop around and try to find the best deal possible for you and your specific circumstances.

However, remember it may not always be just about money. You want to choose a broker with a good reputation and reputable clients that can get the deal done when it's time to close.

It's a good idea to check with other people who have sold credits in that state and see what kind of job their broker did for them. It's always great to get a referral if possible.

The state itself may well have a list of brokers that they work with and recommend – you can just call up the local film commission and ask.

Making A Deal With A Broker

Once you have chosen a broker, you can formalize a deal with them.

It can be smart to organize this before you begin production. That way, you'll have an idea of how much money you're likely to generate from the tax credit sale before you start spending.

By formalizing a deal early, you can lock in a price with a broker and their client, the buyer. This should put your mind at rest and guard against any flexibility in the market by the time you have the tax credit.

This should also give your investors a good idea of how much money they will be recouping once the tax credit is sold. This may also help to attract new investors if you are still putting together the financing.

Indeed, if you are cash-flowing the tax incentive via a bank or financier (as we will discuss shortly), they might insist that you already have a deal in place to sell the tax credit before they agree to provide any kind of production loan. Alternatively, they may look to organize this themselves.

However, at the pre-production stage, the broker will only be able to indicate the price they can get assuming you will do what you say you're going to do.

For example, if you anticipate having the credit by January, and production is delayed and it ends up being June, that might affect the sale price. If the fiscal year in that state ends in April, you will have missed tax season for that year and you may ultimately have to take a lower price.

Or if your qualifying spend ends up being less than what you had budgeted for, that would reduce the final value of your tax credit and might make it less desirable to your broker's clients.

A smart broker will probably build these caveats into their agreement. If you don't meet any of the necessary dates or amounts they require, they may not have to honor the agreed price.

On the flipside, if your broker doesn't come up with the price they agreed to in your contract, you may also be able to renege on the agreement and shop around for a better price if there are no mitigating circumstances.

So, just remember to be flexible, get a good range, and be conservative in your financial planning. Keep your expectations closer to the bottom of the range that the broker says is attainable.

That way, your investors won't get any nasty surprises down the line and, who knows, you may even surpass expectations and give them a bigger check than they had anticipated, which is every producer's dream!

Broker Fees

A tax credit broker will generally charge a small percentage of the total amount of the transaction.

This can vary wildly depending on the amounts and workloads involved. From my experience, a fee of 1% of the total transaction value is usually the starting point.

If you end up with a huge tax credit on your hands, you may be able to cap the maximum amount that the broker can earn from the deal.

Once again, you can shop around to find the best deal you can.

A good broker should be able to oversee the entire transaction for you, alongside any members of your team as necessary, such as your lawyers and accountants. When this is in a state or location far away from where you are based, this can be an invaluable help to you.

When a good broker performs this service well, they will usually justify their fees. They should do much more than simply making an introduction and then letting you and the buyer make a deal.

State Buy-Backs

Certain US states have introduced a system where they will save you the effort of selling the tax credit.

Instead, they will automatically buy the tax credit back from you at a fixed price. No questions, no negotiations, no lawyers, no brokers, no additional fees – easy!

However, they will usually do this at a rate that is a few cents on the dollar less than what a broker might be able to get for you.

For example, let's say a broker tells you they can get you 88 cents on the dollar (so, 88% of the value of the tax credits). That's great, but they might charge you a 1% fee, you might have to spend money on a lawyer to paper the deal, and then you have another party you're answerable to in the mix of everything.

You're also dependent on everybody doing what they say they will do. This includes you, as a producer or filmmaker, being able to deliver the project on time.

As an alternative, the state that you're shooting in might offer you a buy-back system at 83 cents on the dollar. It's less money, but also a lot less of a headache.

If your tax credit is worth $1m, then every cent on the dollar starts to mean a lot more, and that 5c/$ difference adds up to a lot of money. In that case, it may be well worth using a broker to get the maximum cash return possible, even with their commission and some additional fees and work.

But if your tax credit is only worth $100,000, by the time you have paid a broker's commission as well as the legal fees to seal the sale of your tax credit, any additional profits from that 5c/$ higher rate of purchase may just not be worth it.

If that is the case, you may simply prefer to use the state's buy-back option as it is much easier and not a huge difference in terms of the cash amount you'll get back.

It's always worth checking to see whether the location you're filming in offers a buy-back option. You can then make your own calculations and judge what works best for your specific circumstances.

State Transferability

There are some US states that simply don't allow you to transfer their tax credits.

If you cannot transfer (or, in other words, sell) your tax credit to another user, then you could end up with a tax credit certificate on your hands that is of no use or value to you or anyone else.

This makes everything else irrelevant and renders their production tax incentive program next to useless unless a production company is actually based in that state to begin with.

Most states where this was an issue quickly realized this and changed their legislation to allow for the transferability of tax credits.

However, things keep changing. So, before jumping into a location for its tax credit program, just make sure that you can actually sell the certificate on in the first place.

Always check that your tax credit is 'transferable'.

Then, you can worry about the pricing...

Other Restrictions

The issue of state transferability is a big restriction to look out for, but certain locations have other regulations in place that you should be aware of.

These are too numerous to list here but a couple of big ones to look out for include:

- Splitting the credit

    - Some locations will not allow you to sell off the tax credit in smaller chunks. So, if you have a tax credit for $1m, you would have to sell that entire credit or nothing at all

    - Even if you have one buyer that wants to buy $700,000 of credits and another that wants to buy $300,000, the state might not let you split the credit up for those two separate sales. You could only make a single sale of the entire tax credit of $1m

    - Or they may limit you to a maximum number of splits. So, for example, they might not let you divide the tax credit into more than two or three pieces for re-sale

    - This can be very restrictive so always be sure to check the local legislation for this

- Time restrictions

    - Some locations may have very strict regulations about how long an end user has to use a tax credit

    - If, for example, you have a tax credit generated in 2020, some locations might only allow it to be used in 2020, as opposed to 2021 or 2022

    - If your tax credit is generated at the wrong time of year, this can make your certificate much less desirable and you may be forced to sell it at a heavily discounted price to a buyer that can use it at short notice

- Fortunately, most US states now allow at least a couple of years for an end-user to deploy the tax credit certificate, which takes some pressure off the seller

- Just be sure to check any time restrictions your location may have as this could significantly affect the sale price

Case Study

Let's keep things simple and use the same example as we did for our tax rebate earlier, but this time with a tax credit.

We have a film with a $10m budget that we are shooting in a state with a tax credit. Let's assume that we have the same incentive criteria as before:

- 20% tax credit for all qualifying expenses that are made in-state

- Includes both BTL and ATL expenditures

- Includes both resident and non-resident labor

- Does not include any development costs or expenditures made out-of-state

- Additional 10% for any local residents that are hired (so a total of 30% of their salaries)

So, we have gone through our budget line-by-line and noted which expenses qualify and which do not.

We can now see what the face value (or what I call the 'initial gross value') of our tax credit will be, as follows:

BUDGET	$10,000,000		
In-State Qualifying Expenses (excluding Local Hires)	$4,000,000	Tax Credit of 20%	$800,000
Local Hires	$3,000,000	Tax Credit of 30%	$900,000
TOTAL:			**$1,700,000**

According to these calculations, we now expect to get a tax credit certificate worth a total of $1,700,000. So far, it's exactly the same as our earlier example with the tax rebate.

However, in this case, this is just the initial gross value of the tax credit. It is <u>not</u> the final amount that we will receive in cash.

Next Steps

Our goal now is to calculate the net value of the tax credit, which will be the final benefit to the production after all other fees are deducted.

Let's now make a couple more realistic assumptions as follows:

- We find a broker who has a client that is willing to buy our tax credit for 90 cents on the dollar (or 90% of its total value)

- Our broker will sell our tax credit for us for a transaction fee of 1%

    o This fee will be paid out of funds generated by the tax credit sale once the transaction is completed

Now, let's see what that looks like when applied to our example:

TAX CREDIT INITIAL GROSS VALUE		$1,700,000
Client Purchase Price	90%	$1,530,000
Broker Fee	1%	$15,300
TOTAL NET VALUE OF CREDIT:		**$1,514,700**

This means that, from our tax credit certificate worth $1,700,000, we would receive a final cash amount of $1,514,700 back to the production.

We now have a pretty good estimate of what the final net value of our tax credit is going to be once it has been sold and any fees have been deducted.

When you work on your final figures, whether for your finance plan or your recoupment waterfall for your investors, the $1.5147m net figure will be the important one rather than the original $1.7m gross figure.

Additional Costs

As the sale of a tax credit is an official and legal transaction involving state authorities, and given the large figures sometimes involved, you need to be careful to get everything right and keep it above board.

Some producers will want a lawyer to handle the transaction on their behalf to ensure that no detail has been missed. While this is not strictly necessary, it can be a good idea to have someone look over any such documents on your behalf in addition to the broker, who is acting independently. This is particularly the case for large transactions or in locations where the tax incentive program is relatively new.

If you do engage a lawyer, you also need to account for some legal fees in your calculations and deduct them from the final benefit of the tax credit's net value.

You may not need this if, for example, you have a production lawyer that is on retainer, or if your company has an in-house business affairs person that can handle this for you.

Depending on how you have structured your financing, you may also wish to use an escrow account for the transfer of this money, which will incur an additional fee. Just remember to account for these additional expenses when calculating the eventual net benefit of the tax credit.

A Little Extra Effort

You can see from these examples how selling a tax credit is a more complicated process than receiving a tax rebate.

However, tax credits seem to have become more and more popular in US states recently as, in the eyes of the general public at least, it helps to keep their public funding within their tax system, as we discussed earlier.

Many states have increased the rate of their tax credit programs so that, even with the extra costs of selling a tax credit, they are still financially competitive with some of the tax rebate programs that are out there.

Don't be put off by the idea of having to sell the tax credit or working with a broker, even if this does require a little extra effort compared to a more straightforward tax rebate.

In most states, this process has become fairly sophisticated and straightforward, and it can actually be quite simple. The film commissions are set up to help and guide you through this process to make it as smooth as possible. Plenty of producers have done this already with great success, and so can you.

15. Local Requirements

Whether your location's tax incentive program is a rebate or a credit, there will be certain requirements you will need to adhere to so that the process runs smoothly.

Once you have nailed down your location, you will need to consult with the local film commission to make sure you follow all the correct procedures to start the process and then follow them thoroughly until completion.

You may wish to work with a local producer or lawyer as well to help you with this.

Many jurisdictions have a very specific process that you must follow. This shouldn't be too onerous but it is important to make sure that you set things up correctly to avoid any nasty surprises further down the line.

Each location will have their own regulations but here are just a few common things to look out for:

Pre-Certification

Pre-certification is standard in many jurisdictions and is your way of officially registering your production there.

Check to see whether you need to get pre-certified (or equivalent) in your shooting location and, if so, make sure you register everything with the local authorities and get a receipt. Without this, you may not be able to get a tax incentive there, however much money you end up spending.

By getting pre-certified, you and your production will be entered into the film commission's system and thereby serve notice that you will be using their tax incentive program. This will be the first step towards them working with you on an official basis to mount your project there.

To get pre-certified, you will usually need to fill out a form with as many production details as you can, including a budget. You probably won't know every little detail at this early stage but the local film commission will want to see that you are set up to put together a shoot and that they should take you seriously.

The local authorities will use this information to assess how much money they need to set aside for your production once you have wrapped. This may be important if they have a tight budget or their tax incentive program has a yearly cap that they cannot exceed.

Remember, once you are pre-certified for a certain amount, that is the number that will have been set aside for you. That number can go down but, in jurisdictions where their budget is tight, it might not go up.

For example, if a jurisdiction has assigned $1m to your film, and you end up spending more than you anticipated and generate a tax credit of $1.5m, that jurisdiction may not have the available funds to make up that additional $500,000 above what has already been earmarked to you.

So, if you're not sure where things will fall, err on the side of 'slightly higher' rather than 'slightly lower' in your pre-certification submission documents. The key word is 'slightly' – you should still be realistic in your projections. If the governing body finds your numbers to be unrealistic, they may question your credibility.

Usually, the pre-certification commitments made by a location will expire at a certain point. For example, a location might state that if you have not begun production within 90 or 180 days of being officially pre-certified, you will lose your funding allocation and will have to re-apply.

This will then open up those funds for another production that may be ready to shoot sooner.

You may need to pay a fee or put down a refundable deposit to be pre-certified. This will usually be only a modest amount, or it might be a percentage of the expected tax incentive amount, which will usually be capped at something quite affordable.

This is to encourage only serious productions to apply so that, if a jurisdiction has limited funds to assign, it doesn't tie up all these funds with productions that might never happen.

Setting Up An SPV

Whether or not it is required by the local legislation, you will likely end up forming a new company incorporated in your chosen location.

This SPV will act as your project's production company. It will be a legal entity and all your local deals will go through that SPV.

This is usually a fairly straightforward process that has been done a million times before, so don't be scared off by this.

However, some locations require you to have a very specific corporate structure in order to apply for and receive their tax incentive.

Check to see whether there are any logistical requirements that you must meet. You can then feel confident knowing that you have set up your SPV in the correct way.

The SPV may also need to file a local tax return in the jurisdiction in which you are shooting. It's a great idea to work with a local lawyer, accountant or producer that has been through this process before to guide you in the best and most cost-effective way to get this done.

Audit

While practically every jurisdiction you shoot in will want to study your books and receipts before granting you an incentive, some may require an official state-sponsored audit.

If they do require an audit, this could add some costs for a local accounting firm that you might be responsible for, so you must allow for this in your budget.

It may also require you to keep your books, and conduct your accounting, in a specific way.

An audit can add significantly to the time it takes for the local authorities to generate your tax incentive. Depending on their requirements, an audit can take weeks or even months, which can affect your bottom line if you are cash-flowing the incentive (as we discuss later).

So, it's advisable to check whether there is an audit requirement beforehand so that you can prepare sufficiently and be ready for it when the time arrives.

Credits And Logo

Most jurisdictions will require you to include a specific credit or mention for them in the finished product. After all, they want to promote business in their city, state or country, and this is a prime opportunity for them to show their contribution towards your production.

This should be pretty straightforward. It is usually just a credit on the end roll, possibly accompanied by their logo.

On some rare occasions, the location may request individual credits for one or more of their executives. This is fairly rare though, and the local film commission would have to do something quite extraordinary to justify this in the opinion of most producers.

Make sure you have the exact wording that you need to include well ahead of time. The film commission should have a standard text that they can provide you with.

This shouldn't be a tough requirement for you to meet. Just make sure you don't forget to do it!

Content Review And Finished Product

Many places will have requirements related to the type of productions and content that you can shoot there to generate a tax incentive.

While feature films and TV shows are accepted in practically every tax incentive program around the world, the situation is not always so clear for short films, music videos, web series, commercials, and other types of productions.

And as far as the content itself is concerned, some locations have restrictions on that too.

For example, many places will not offer you a tax incentive for any content that they consider to be pornographic, no matter how much money you spend there.

Even if you are not shooting a strictly pornographic film, if you are shooting in an area with a particular religious or cultural sensitivity, they may still deny your application on the basis of excessive or gratuitous nudity, violence or swearing.

Certain cultures hold different views than what you might be used to. So, they may not respond so well to content concerning death or the afterlife (featured in many horror or zombie films), or magic and wizardry (featured in many fantasy films and TV shows).

Some locations may simply not qualify you for any content that is 'R'-rated.

Don't take these cultural sensitivities for granted. You should establish from an early stage whether your production is going to infringe on anything thematically that might ultimately deny you a tax incentive.

If there is a pre-certification process, you will probably be required to describe your production, including a logline. You may even be required to provide a script for them to review.

If you are approved at this early stage – and you don't deviate too much from this plan! – you shouldn't have any problems once the production is complete.

However, some jurisdictions may request a copy of the finished product to review before they sign off on the tax incentive to make sure that there is no content in there that falls foul of their regulations. While this may be standard, you do not want this to be nerve-wracking!

This will also be their opportunity to ensure that you have included their logo, credits or any other requirements they may have.

If a jurisdiction requires a finished copy of your film or TV show to process the tax incentive, you won't get your tax credit or rebate until after you have finished post-production. If you are cash-flowing your tax incentive and accumulating interest on a loan, or you have investors waiting for this money, you will need to account for this in your financing and recoupment projections.

If you have any doubt about a location's content requirements, ask the local film commission directly and make sure that your production will qualify for their incentive program.

Distribution

While less common, some locations might want to see some form of distribution in place for your project before they can guarantee you their tax incentive.

This can be notoriously difficult for a smaller independent project, where pre-sale contracts with distributors can be harder to come by.

This is usually a not-so-subtle way for a region to tell filmmakers that they want to use their tax incentive money to attract big studio movies and TV shows. Studios have their own distribution platforms so this requirement will not present a problem for them.

Such locations may have a small or new infrastructure and don't have the capacity to deal with lots of smaller independent productions. Instead they would prefer a few big studio productions to take advantage of the funds they have available. This is less work for them, and usually more prestigious too.

Fortunately, even where there is a distribution requirement, the film commission might be flexible on what they need to see from you. Often a sales agency agreement will suffice rather than a string of distribution contracts in territories across the world. This is much more achievable.

They will just want to feel confident that this project will get distributed and be seen by audiences, which will more easily allow them to market themselves as a shooting location and a place to do business.

Again, you will just need to check whether this is a requirement with the film commission before you commit to shooting there and, if so, whether there is a way for you to comply. They will likely try to find a way to work with you and keep everyone happy.

Minimum Requirements

Many locations will require you to meet certain minimums to qualify for their tax incentive program.

These might include:

- Minimum spend

    o You may be required to spend at least a certain amount of money on qualifying local expenditures

- Minimum days

    o You may be required to spend at least a certain number of days, either in production or post-production, in the location

- Minimum percentage

    o You may have to meet a requirement of minimum spend or minimum days but this time expressed as a percentage of your overall budget or shoot

- Minimum budget

    o Some locations only want productions of a certain size to qualify for their resources, irrespective of how much of it is shot in their location

- Minimum residents employed

    o You may have to hire a certain number of local residents or spend a certain amount of money on local hires

These are just a few examples of some of the minimum requirements that some locations may need you to meet.

These are usually in place to prevent producers from coming in to a location for comparatively negligible expenditures and still claiming a tax incentive, despite not really impacting the local economy.

An example would be if you went to a location to shoot a few days of B-roll, or to record a couple of days of ADR with a certain actor. In these cases, your primary shooting location is clearly somewhere else. If you are not actually basing your production there, these locations may prefer to direct their limited resources elsewhere.

This also prevents you from 'double-dipping', which is the process of claiming two different tax incentives on the same production. There are legitimate ways of doing this, such as by mounting an international co-production (which we discuss later in this book), but aside from that, the practice is generally discouraged by locations setting minimum requirements in the ways described here.

If you plan to shoot in a location that has such minimum requirements, you will need to make sure that you can meet these when creating your budget and schedule.

Caps

Equally, many locations have caps (or maximums) built into their tax incentive programs.

These might include:

- Program cap

    o A jurisdiction may only have been allocated a certain amount of funding from their annual budget to dedicate to their production tax incentive program

- Once this annual cap has been reached, there will be no more funds left and they will no longer be able to grant a tax incentive to any new productions until the following year

- 'Per production' cap

    - There may be a maximum value of tax incentive that a single production can be granted, irrespective of how much your qualifying spend amounts to

    - For example, a location may have a 'per production' cap of $500,000, meaning that whether you spend $10m or $100m in that location, the final tax incentive amount for a single project will never be more than $500,000

- Individual item cap

    - There may be a maximum value of any individual item that can be claimed for the tax incentive – this is particularly common for large salaries

    - For example, it may be that you cannot claim more than $100,000 for any individual's salary, whether that individual earns $500,000 or $5m

These are just a few examples but there may be many more. All of these factors could be extremely significant.

If the program is capped, you will need an assurance that there will be sufficient funds available for you before you start production.

This is where pre-certification can be useful. If there are only limited funds available for production incentives that year, you should have a certain amount already allocated to you before you start spending money there.

However, you should never simply assume that the money will be available for you if the program has a cap. Always try to get a very clear assurance (in writing, if possible) from the local film commission that the necessary funds will be available before committing to that location. If there is any doubt about that, then you may have to re-consider shooting there.

If there is a 'per production' cap, this means that there can only be a certain amount of funding allocated to any one production. So, whether your qualifying spend is $10m or $100m, you may end up receiving the same tax incentive due to that location's production caps.

That's a huge amount of money that you could be leaving on the table! If your budget is on the higher end, you may be better off looking for a program that does not have a 'per production' cap.

If there is an individual item cap, this could affect your big-ticket items especially.

If, for example, you are paying your star a $3m salary, and the incentive program has an individual item cap of $1m, that means that you can only claim the incentive on the first $1m of that star's salary. That's $2m that won't qualify – a significant amount.

In all cases, be sure to check your location's minimums and caps. Apply these carefully to all your figures, and make sure that they will work for your specific circumstances.

For this reason, some less-restrictive locations are better for the bigger studio tentpoles and TV series with huge budgets and massive individual salaries, while others that have certain caps in place are more suitable for lower-budget indie movies.

You just have to pick the one that works best for you. And remember, just because a location worked well for one producer, or for your last production, that doesn't mean that it will automatically be suitable for your next one given that your budget and financing requirements are probably completely different.

16. Local Infrastructure

Even the best tax incentive program in the world isn't a sole reason to choose a certain location for your film or TV show.

While hugely important, it must be combined with a number of other factors when making your final decision. Remember the practicalities of your production and what you will need for it to run smoothly on a day-to-day basis once you are there.

In fact, sometimes a great tax incentive can mask certain issues with the local infrastructure.

Some places will offer an enormous incentive precisely because they can't offer the same services as other locations. These large tax incentives are sometimes designed to compensate for the additional costs of bringing in extra equipment and personnel.

If that is the case, is it really worth the extra work and effort of going there for not much additional benefit?

It's important to do some research, ask around to see who has shot there before, and get a good feel for the local infrastructure on your location scouts.

Some questions you may need to consider include:

Are There Enough Local Crews Available?

Most tax incentives will reward you for hiring local resident crew members that are based in their region.

But, as we've already mentioned, remember to research thoroughly how likely it is that those local crews will actually be available.

You can go to a place with a great incentive only to find that a few big studio movies are also shooting there at the same time and there is no local crew left for you to hire.

Suddenly you need to bring in non-local crews from another location. Not only might their salaries not count as qualifying spend for the incentive as you had planned, but they will also cost more to travel in and put up in hotels, as well as per diems and all sorts of other costs that can raise your budget.

While these extra costs themselves may count as qualifying spend, it is unlikely that they will match the salary that you were previously hoping could be included.

As such, a significant benefit of the tax incentive may be eroded, as well as pushing your basic costs up.

Are The Crews Of A High Standard?

Even if there are local crew members available, you shouldn't take for granted that they can work to the standard and schedule that you need.

Particularly if you are shooting in a foreign country, these crew members may have been trained differently, or they may be used to working at a different level or speed than what you are used to back home.

Cultural differences may also surprise you if you are not prepared. In some cultures, workers might expect to be granted more breaks or for longer periods of time than what you are used to. If you are going to their region, it's likely that you will have to adapt to their customs rather than the other way round.

Fortunately, as productions continue to ramp up in non-traditional shooting locations, the quality levels of the local crews have improved dramatically, and basic international standards are increasingly settled upon.

However, it is always a good idea to speak to other producers and filmmakers that have shot there recently to ensure that the local crews will be able to perform at the level that you are expecting.

Are There Enough High-Quality Amenities To Suit Your Needs?

Some non-traditional shooting locations run before they can walk in their appetites to attract big productions to their region.

This means that, occasionally, their infrastructure struggles to keep up with the demands placed on it by the tax incentive program.

For example, you might find yourself shooting somewhere that is quite remote and simply doesn't have enough quality hotels and accommodations available for all the cast and crew that you will be bringing from Los Angeles or London, where they are used to a certain level of comfort.

It can take well over a year to build a new hotel, let alone train the staff and get everything right. **A sudden influx of productions early into a region's tax incentive program can simply overwhelm what limited resources it has available, a fact that its governing body may not have fully considered.**

The same goes for the amenities available, such as restaurants and catering. Again, consider what your cast and crew are used to in their daily lives. If they hear that amenities of the level to which they are accustomed are simply not available in your shooting location, this could deter them from signing on to your production.

These may seem like minor issues, but they are ones that we have all lived through. When people are staying in a bad hotel or eating bad food, they can become grumpy and less productive, leading to an unhappy set and working environment in which everyone suffers, including the overall quality of your final product.

This applies to transportation too. You should always make sure that your cast and crew can be transported to and from the set easily every day. If not, your shoot may turn into a logistical nightmare where people miss their call times and you incur significant production delays and, consequently, additional costs.

Make sure that there are car and bus services – luxury services where necessary – to ensure that everyone can get where they need to be and on time.

Most of these issues can be addressed during your location scout. It's always worth taking some time to scout out the area beyond your specific shooting locations and looking carefully at the hotels and restaurants that are available locally.

The film commission should also be able to point you in the right direction here, but nothing beats the first-hand knowledge that you get from seeing this with your own eyes.

Is There Enough Entertainment To Keep People Occupied On Their Days Off?

If your cast and crew begin to get restless on their days off, they may find other ways of distracting themselves.

This might not always bode well for your production.

When people grow idle and bored, they can sometimes find themselves getting into trouble. This is especially true when they are immersed in a foreign country or culture they are not used to.

This can create the wrong kind of headlines and bring negative publicity to your project, as well as bringing disruption to the actual filmmaking experience.

If you are shooting in the middle of nowhere, you will need to think about what people will be doing with themselves rather than being stuck in a hotel room and getting agitated.

Is There So Much Going On That They Will Be Distracted?

Conversely, you may find yourself shooting in a place with far too much temptation for certain members of your cast and crew.

Producers are not parents, and your crew members are not kids that need looking after, but, at the same time, you need to run a disciplined and well-oiled set.

Shooting in a location where crazy nightlife and attractions abound can make it difficult to manage when you are relying on a hundred people to turn up on set early the following morning.

Much of this comes down to the personnel you employ and how reliable they are – some people will find trouble wherever they go, no matter how big or small the location!

But if you are putting up a large out-of-town cast and crew including many young people, be aware that the bright lights of a big new city can be a distraction.

Is It Safe?

You will ultimately be responsible for the safety of your cast and crew.

If you end up shooting in a far-off location that you are not familiar with, make sure it does not have a bad reputation where your cast and crew might find themselves in dangerous situations where they become a target.

If you have any doubts about the safety of that location, you may need to hire additional security, which must be factored into your budget.

This also makes for an unpleasant shooting experience for all involved. You will have enough to think about during production without worrying about the safety of crew members, high-profile cast, and expensive equipment.

Shooting in a location that has a reputation for being unsafe may also deter cast and crew members who are considering whether to join your production.

Will All The Facilities You Need Be Available?

Does the location have all the stages that you need? If you are planning on doing any kind of post-production there, are those facilities available too? How about equipment?

Don't take any of this for granted. It should be fairly easy to do the necessary research and find out what is available and when in that location.

As with crews, do not underestimate the number of equipment rentals or sound stages that exist in that location and what their availability will be like during your intended production period.

If a big studio production is in town, they may have simply booked up all the local stages and you are left shooting in some warehouse near an airport. Not good!

If equipment is not available locally, you may be able to bring this in from elsewhere, but it will be at some expense and the costs of doing so may not count towards the tax incentive.

So, when on your location scout, it's very important to view all the possible facilities that you might need to get a good idea of what will be available locally, including your second-, third- and fourth-choice options.

How Do You Deal With The Local Unions?

Wherever you go, cast and crew members may be protected by their local unions. This means that you will have to deal with these unions and adhere to their very strict guidelines on what their members require during your production.

In the US, some states are unionized, while other states are 'right-to-work' states.

In these 'right-to-work' states, in theory you don't have to worry about certain unions. However, even in those states, you may need to make a deal with some of them, particularly if you are bringing in crew from a different state.

And in some states that are unionized, the union rules are particularly strict, which can increase your costs in ways you may not have accounted for.

Again, it's a good idea to talk to other producers and filmmakers who have shot similar productions in that location and see what kind of issues, if any, they had to deal with from the unions.

That way you can be most prepared and leave enough wiggle room in your budget for any extra costs that you may not have originally anticipated.

PART THREE

17. Now What?

By this point in the process, a lot of hard work has been done, and a lot of tough decisions have been made.

You've finally found the right location for your production, you've broken down your budget with your producer, you've worked through the local legislation with your team, you know what your qualifying spend is likely to be, and you now have an accurate idea of what your tax incentive is going to be worth by the end of production.

For a lot of people, that's about as far as you need to go. Now the hard work of actually making your film or TV show begins, making sure you spend the money like you said you were going to, and complying with all the local legislation along the way.

That way, you can make sure that the tax incentive you get back at the end of the process will be pretty close to what you had predicted, and there aren't any big surprises in store for you.

If your production is backed by a studio or equity financiers, you can simply build the likely returns from the tax incentive into your recoupment plan.

You can tell your investors that, once the tax incentive is generated, they can expect to start seeing some income and are less reliant on other forms of revenue (such as a film's box office performance) to break even and then turn a profit.

The tax incentive is therefore a major source of recoupment for your investors.

But what if you're not backed by a studio, or don't have enough equity finance to get you through the production?

For a lot of independent movies in particular, this is a common problem.

The answer, for many, is to 'cash-flow' the tax incentive and get that money up-front for use during the production itself.

Let's take a look at how that process works...

18. Cash-Flowing Your Tax Incentive

Now that you understand how tax incentives work, we can talk about how you can use them to help finance your production.

What Does 'Cash-Flowing A Tax Incentive' Mean?

Cash-flowing (or banking) a tax incentive describes the process of obtaining financing (usually in the form of a loan) secured uniquely against the tax incentive. The money generated by the loan can then be used for your production expenses.

This is a form of 'debt financing', where a financier is investing against a specific security.

This is different from equity financing, where the equity investors are dependent on the film or TV show actually becoming profitable for them to make their money back (which we discuss in more detail in another book in this series).

Cash-flowing a tax incentive might be a familiar process for anyone that has ever obtained a loan from a bank before.

The bank (or another financier or lender) would be willing to give you a loan provided it is secured against a certain piece of collateral. They will thoroughly examine that collateral to be comfortable that its value will protect their investment.

They will then lend you some money, which you will need to pay back at a later date under certain conditions. They will also charge some fees and interest to make it worth their while.

It's a bit like when you get a mortgage on a house you want to buy. The bank will appraise the property and make a detailed assessment about what they think the correct value of the house is, and then decide how much they are willing to lend you secured against the house as collateral. You would agree to certain fees and interest rates and – voila! – the house is yours.

Cash-flowing a tax incentive follows a similar principle (albeit with a different repayment structure). In this case, instead of a house, the collateral is the tax incentive itself.

So, a lender will calculate how much the tax incentive will be worth (just as we did previously) and then – hopefully! – lend you that amount of money, minus any discounts, fees and interest that they plan on charging.

Once production is complete and the tax incentive is generated, the lender will recoup all the money that they are owed.

Then, if any additional money generated by the tax incentive is left over once the lender is fully paid back, the production gets to keep it.

Who Can Cash-Flow My Tax Incentive?

Any investor can cash-flow your tax incentive.

In fact, for some investors, they would much prefer to cash-flow a tax incentive than invest in an equity position. The rewards are potentially lower but so is the risk, and some investors prefer this more cautious approach.

As investments in film or TV go, cash-flowing a tax incentive is generally regarded as being one of the least risky forms of investing.

That's because tax incentives are backed by a public governmental body such as a country or a state. Such public bodies are usually seen as less likely to default on their obligations than a private corporation or individual.

If you can find an individual investor that wants to cash-flow a tax incentive themselves, you can strike any kind of deal you want and negotiate the best terms for yourself.

Most producers, however, will look to a more established financier to cash-flow their tax incentives.

This will most commonly be one of two types of company:

- A bank

    o Many banks have entertainment divisions specifically to handle these kinds of deals

- A boutique entertainment financier with its own private source of funds

This is now a sophisticated industry, and the banks and financiers are in a competitive marketplace trying to get your business.

This is great news for a producer! It has led to rates being extremely competitive and allows you to shop around for the best deal.

Having a bank or financier cash-flow your tax incentive also allows you to get an injection of cash into your project without giving away any equity.

A bank or financier will not usually take any significant kind of profit participation position in the recoupment waterfall when they cash-flow a tax incentive.

Or, to put it simply, even if your film makes a billion dollars at the box office, the financier will rarely enjoy much of that because their transaction has been a simple fee-based loan. Once they have been paid back their principal loan amount, as well as their fees and interest, the financier should be out of the deal.

If a debt financier does insist on some kind of equity position, it will usually be because their risk when cash-flowing your tax incentive is higher than it would normally be, or to compensate for particularly low interest rates.

Otherwise, any equity position granted to the tax incentive financier should be fairly nominal.

Equity investors usually like this. It means that they can invest less money into the project but retain the same portion of back-end. Even though the production will have to pay some fees to cash-flow the tax incentive, investors will usually be fine with this if they really believe that they can make some money at the box office or via distribution contracts.

If the project does make millions of dollars, they will want to share those profits with as few other parties as possible.

How Much Does This Cost?

These deals will usually look like a regular bank loan in their fee structures.

Every deal is different and every company works in a different way, but typically you can expect to be charged the following:

- An up-front facility fee

- An interest rate

The fee levels will usually be associated with the perceived risk of this investment by the financier. We will talk about some of the major potential risk factors involved in cash-flowing a tax incentive shortly.

Your financier will consider all these risk factors when setting their fees.

The fees will also depend on the 'term' of the loan. This is the length of the loan and how long you will have to pay it back.

Paying The Fees And Interest

Many producers worry that they will have to pay these fees out of their own pocket. However, that's not usually how such a loan is set up.

The most common scenario is that the bank or financier will include these fees in the gross loan amount that they are lending you. They would calculate what they think the total amount of fees and interest will be, and then deduct that number from the amount that they advance to the production.

So, for example, if you were borrowing $1m, only $900,000 may actually go into your production account. The remaining $100,000 would be held back to cover the fees and interest you will owe.

You would, however, be paying interest on that full $1m amount, which is the total value of the 'loan facility'.

This will mean slightly less cash going towards the production itself, but it takes the financial pressure off you as a producer and keeps the lender happy as well.

Interest Reserve

Depending on the circumstances, the financier may elect to create an 'interest reserve'. This is a separate bank account that would be formed to hold the amount of interest due on the loan.

So, however much the financier anticipates being owed to them in fees, they will simply deposit that amount into the interest reserve account.

As time ticks by, the interest on the amount that has been drawn down will be calculated and then transferred back to the lender from the interest reserve on a monthly basis (unless negotiated otherwise).

Although this sounds like a complex structure, it is primarily an accounting mechanism that some banks and financiers prefer. You should just be aware of the basics of how an interest reserve works in case you see this in your loan documents.

Turnaround Time

When embarking on this process, it is essential to understand how long it will take for the jurisdiction's governing body to issue your rebate check or credit certificate once you have submitted all the necessary documentation. This process is sometimes referred to as the 'turnaround time'.

This is a <u>vital</u> question to ask a film commission when committing to their tax incentive program, even if you are not cash-flowing it. Some jurisdictions take longer than others to process their tax incentives. Do not assume that they will automatically process your rebate check or tax credit right away. Have a clear idea of the official turnaround time, and then check with other producers that have worked there as to how accurate this is.

Some jurisdictions process their incentives quickly, within a month or two of receiving a production's books and documents. Others clearly state that it can take six months or more for the incentive to be issued. There are even some jurisdictions that split their incentive check or certificate over two or more years, depending on its size.

This is a variable that can leave some producers feeling surprised or unprepared. However, the turnaround time should be clear in the legislation.

Knowing the turnaround time is vital when defining the term of a loan, which in turn will affect the level of fees and interest that is being calculated and possibly put into an interest reserve. Even if you are not cash-flowing your incentive with a bank, your investors will also want to know the turnaround time of the tax incentive to calculate their own recoupment schedules.

So, make sure that you are in the know!

Late Fees And Penalties

Of course, as with any loan, if you do not pay back what you owe to the financier (the principal loan amount, plus any fees and interest) within the term that you have agreed, they will likely charge you late fees and penalties.

This is where the loan can get really expensive. Most likely, your monthly rate of interest will shoot up. This could be a 50% increase or even more.

So, for example, you may have a loan with a term of 12 months at 10% annual interest paid monthly.

Once that term of 12 months expires, you may suddenly find yourself having to pay an interest rate of 15% as a penalty for being late.

This is why it is so important to have a really good idea of how long it will take for the tax incentive to be generated. Only then can you establish a realistic term for the loan and an appropriate interest reserve to ensure that additional fees and penalties for late payment are unlikely.

If a film commission tells you it will take them 6 months to generate your tax incentive once production is complete, you need to factor that in when establishing the term of your loan. Maybe, in that case, an 18-month term is more appropriate than a 12-month loan, even though that means a larger interest payment and less money to the production.

This is the best way to protect yourself and your production here.

If the interest reserve account runs out of money and you still owe the lender, they may be entitled to recoup what they are owed in a preferential position from any future revenues you make, notably from distribution. This will leave your other investors very unhappy, so it is a scenario you want to avoid.

However, this is something that nobody wants, including the financier. They don't want to charge you late fees and penalties and have to scramble around with other investors to get repaid their money. They would much prefer to get their loan repaid on time, charge whatever fees they are due, and re-invest this money into another deal.

So, if the financier has any doubts about your ability to repay the loan, chances are they simply won't lend to you in the first place.

Legal Fees And Logistics

Before going to a financier to cash-flow your tax incentive, be aware that they will need to conduct a careful analysis of your numbers to make sure they agree with them.

There may be a lot of due diligence. Producers are sometimes caught off guard by the level of thoroughness that some of these financiers go through.

Once again, just imagine going into a bank and asking for any other kind of loan or investment. For them, it's all about the bottom line.

The financier likely won't get all excited about which stars you have attached or where the film or TV show will be premiering. They will get excited, however, at the prospect of making some money.

They will therefore need to put in place the right contracts and paperwork to secure their position against the tax incentive once it is generated. Unfortunately, that usually means lawyers and the fees that they charge.

Legal fees are the bit that nobody likes (except the lawyers). The financier will usually insist that their legal fees are paid by the production. These legal fees will either be added to your bill or they will be deducted from the gross amount of the loan so that you won't be out-of-pocket.

Using a financier that is used to doing these deals, particularly in the jurisdiction that you are planning to shoot in, will help significantly. They will already know the requirements for that particular program, which keeps expectations and fees at a manageable level. They may even have contacts at the local film commission or tax authorities that they can call if they need specific information urgently.

They may also be able to re-use some of the same paperwork from their last deal there. This could save a lot of money in legal fees as a lawyer will not need to draft those documents afresh.

Always ask whether your financier has worked in your shooting location and with your tax incentive program previously, and see whether that might be helpful. And, when negotiating with them, try to establish what their legal and analysis fees will likely be, and whether you can cap them at a certain number.

Independent Analysis

As we've already discussed, you and your line producer will have made your own calculations about how much the tax incentive will likely be worth.

Unfortunately, most financiers aren't all that trusting when it comes to other people handling their money.

For this reason, most lenders and financiers will either make their own calculations or employ the services of an independent analyst to do so on their behalf.

This analyst will go through each line of the budget and, based on their own experience, coupled with their expert knowledge of that tax incentive program and the local infrastructure, they will make their own calculation of what they believe the incentive will ultimately be worth.

Although this might seem frustrating, having an independent analysis could prove helpful to you as a producer. If the analyst's numbers are very different from your own calculations, they may be able to liaise directly with your line producer to make sure that they are doing their job correctly and haven't missed anything.

Your line producer should have the chance to explain to the analyst any critical assumptions they have made to arrive at the figure they have. The analyst should in turn be able to work with your line producer and highlight any areas where they could be doing more to maximize the tax incentive or, conversely, where they have overestimated their ability to get certain local hires or equipment.

All of this will help you in the long run to eliminate many nasty surprises further down the line when it is too late to remedy them.

In fact, even productions that are not cash-flowing their tax incentives with a financier will often still employ an independent analyst to work with them to maximize their incentive and ensure that their expectations are realistic.

The bad news is that the production will usually have to foot the bill for this analysis, even though it is a requirement of the financier.

This, like everything, is up for negotiation, but don't be surprised if an additional fee is placed on the financing for this.

The price will vary depending on the level of service that the analyst provides. If they are simply crunching some numbers then it shouldn't be too expensive, but if they really need to get involved on your behalf and start liaising with the local film commissions then it could go way up.

Having an independent analysis is usually to everyone's benefit. If the tax incentive ends up coming in at significantly less than what was anticipated, the fact that the lender did their own analysis can protect the production legally from any accusations of misrepresentation, providing you did what you said you were going to do and stuck to your budget.

Discount

Even with an independent analysis, there will always be changes and expenses that are simply impossible to anticipate. For this reason, most lenders will take your projected tax incentive number and apply a discount to it in case of an underspend.

In this case, an underspend is when you end up spending less money on qualifying expenses than you had anticipated.

Let's say you had assumed that you would spend $1m on local crew, all of which would qualify for the tax incentive. If half of that crew suddenly isn't available and you have to bring in crew from another state, now you might only be spending $500,000 on local crew, while the rest of the crew's salaries don't qualify for the tax incentive as they are not local.

This means you now have an underspend of $500,000, and that will significantly reduce the amount of your tax incentive.

To protect themselves against this, the lender will typically apply a discount to your anticipated tax incentive amount. This will usually be around 10% but could be more if, for example, you don't have a track record as a producer and still need to prove your reliability.

So, let's say you have a tax rebate estimated to be worth $1m. A financier might automatically apply a 10% discount in case your qualifying spend is less than what you had forecast. This means that, before even calculating any fees and interest, the maximum amount that they would lend you would be $900,000.

We talk about this in more detail shortly when discussing the risks associated with cash-flowing a tax incentive.

For now though, it is simply important to note that the financier will almost always look to be conservative. So, if there is ever a question mark about whether an item will qualify, they will probably assume it won't. And even once they have established their final numbers, they will assume that some of the predictions of what will ultimately qualify will end up being incorrect or less than expected.

For this reason, they may immediately apply this discount to give them a level of comfort and a buffer against any unpleasant surprises.

Financial Closing

When dealing with any kind of debt financing, particularly from a bank or lending institution, you will likely be subject to a financial closing.

This refers to the moment when all the sources of financing for a production are in place, all terms are agreed and documents are signed, and it's finally time for everyone to transfer their money.

The financier will want to see that all your other sources of financing are ready to fund. They may even require that all the other money has been placed into the production account already or, alternatively, into an escrow account and is just waiting to be released.

Then, and only then, will their money be transferred into the production account, whether from an escrow account or from the account of each financier.

This process is known as a financial closing. If you have a completion bond in place (which we discuss a little later), then the bond company might help oversee and regulate this process.

This means that, apart from any development financing or private equity that you may have raised earlier in the process, you likely won't receive the rest of your production funding until everything is set up, agreed, and in place.

You won't, for example, be able to get the tax incentive money first to fund your pre-production until you can raise the rest of the financing. Producers ask me that all the time but it just doesn't work like that!

The risk that the project never materializes is too great and most banks and financiers simply won't put up their money until they see that the budget is fully funded at a financial closing.

How Does The Lender Get Paid Back?

The lender gets paid back once the tax incentive is generated. They will stand in 'first position' to receive any money that they are owed from the rebate check or tax credit once it is sold.

This will usually be detailed in a bunch of legal documents, and you will be legally obliged to pay them from the incentive proceeds. There will be no wiggle room or negotiation on this.

The production may elect to use a collection account for the receipt of any incoming revenues, including those generated by the tax incentive. Indeed, for some debt financiers this may be an obligation. This is a bit like an escrow account, and serves as a neutral third party bank account. We discuss collection accounts in detail in another book in this series on sales and distribution.

If the production is using a collection account, the money can be sent there, and the correct amount then distributed to the financier. This keeps things transparent and clean.

If there is no collection account, the tax incentive proceeds will likely be sent directly to the production account and you will be responsible for transferring the correct amount on to the lender.

If you are found to have received the tax incentive money and not paid it back to the lender as you are contractually obliged, you could get into serious trouble.

Not only will this likely incur penalties and additional costs for you due to breach of contract, in some cases it may also be seen as fraud or another financial crime. This would damage your reputation as a producer or filmmaker, not to mention the fact that you could face prosecution, or the production company could have action taken against it and you could lose control of the title. It is not something you want to risk, ever!

Assigning The Tax Incentive

Where possible, the financier might look for the tax rebate or credit to be assigned directly to them. This means that, once the money is generated, it will be sent directly to the financier, rather than relying on the producers to distribute that money.

In that case, if there is any additional money left over from the tax incentive proceeds once the financier is paid out, they would then be obliged to transfer this to you.

Some states and jurisdictions allow for the assignment of the tax incentive and some don't. It would be a question of checking with the local film commission on their legislation for this.

Banking Restrictions

It is worth noting that many traditional banks and financiers have guidelines in place as to the types of deals that they will do and the people with whom they will work.

Many of the larger banks and financiers may have a minimum amount for any loans that they make.

For them, the time and effort that is spent processing a loan must be justified by the fees that they can earn from it. If the loan amount is too small, then many banks will simply say that it is not worth all the paperwork, legal fees and manpower that they have to dedicate to the process for such a minimal return. They would likely prefer to deploy that money as part of a larger deal instead.

So, if you are a small independent film with a tax incentive of, for example, $50,000 that needs to be cash-flowed, many of the larger banks or financiers will say that this is simply not worth their time.

If that's you, don't worry – there will likely still be other investors or even boutique financiers out there who may be willing to cash-flow your tax incentive, or who will build it into their recoupment plan as part of an equity investment.

And you never know, maybe one of the bigger banks will want to start a relationship with you and will take on the loan. Even if it is a small amount, they may already have documentation from a previous deal that they can re-use, and they may view this as a low-risk deal with a quick turnaround time. So just ask! You might be pleasantly surprised.

Certain financiers will also have guidelines as to the track records of the producers and filmmakers to whom they are willing to lend. Generally, a good deal is a good deal, so you shouldn't worry too much about this now. But some lenders do prefer investing in producers and filmmakers that already have a track record of getting projects completed and delivered.

So again, if you're just starting out, try not to take it personally if one of the bigger banks shies away from financing your first deal. There should still be plenty of financiers out there that are willing to work with you – you may just have to look a little harder to find them.

If a bank does have doubts about you, there will also be other measures that you can put in place to reassure them, such as a completion bond (as we discuss shortly) and an experienced team around you.

So, do your research, and be realistic in your expectations when building your finance plan. But also know that there will always be possibilities out there, even if the most obvious route is blocked at first.

19. Case Study

Let's take our previous examples of both a tax rebate and a tax credit and imagine we are going to cash-flow them.

This process might look as follows:

Tax Rebate

As per our original example, we have a tax rebate with a projected gross value of $1.7m.

If you remember, this is what we had previously calculated for our $10m budget film once we had broken down its qualifying spend.

Our aim in getting that tax rebate cash-flowed is to get as much of that money as possible up-front for use during our production.

So, we would take all our documentation to a few lenders and financiers, whether they are banks or private finance companies, and see who can offer us the best deal in terms of their fee structure and rates.

For the sake of this example, let's assume that we accept an offer from a bank with the following terms:

- 10% discount on the projected gross value of the tax rebate
- 2.5% up-front fee (also known as a 'facility fee')
- 8% p.a. ('per annum', or per year) rate of interest

- 18-month term

    o The anticipated total amount of interest is calculated by taking the monthly interest payment on your loan and multiplying it by the number of months in the term

- $10,000 legal fees

That would give us a calculation as follows:

Projected Gross Value of Tax Rebate		$1,700,000
Discount (in case of underspend)	10%	$170,000
Discounted Amount to be Cash-Flowed / Loan Facility Amount		$1,530,000
Up-Front Fee	2.5%	$38,250
Rate of Interest	8% p.a.	
Term	18 months	
Projected Interest		$183,600
Legal Fees		$10,000
NET AMOUNT TO PRODUCTION		$1,298,150

So, according to these calculations, the bank will set up a loan facility of $1,530,000. This is also the number they will be charging us interest on.

Once they have applied the necessary deductions, as well as their fees and projected interest, the cash amount that they will be injecting into the production up-front is $1,298,150.

Then, once our production is complete and the tax rebate is generated, we would need to pay the bank back the full amount of their loan from the money we receive. In this case, that would be $1,530,000.

If our tax rebate ends up being $1.7m as initially projected, the production gets to keep any money that is left over once the bank is fully paid out.

As you can see, this cash-flowing structure would bring the net value of our tax rebate for cash-flow purposes down from where we started with the gross amount. However, this is still an injection of nearly $1.3m cash that we would otherwise not have had.

All such deals are structured differently, so you may find a financier that employs a more flexible financing model. However, the model shown here is pretty standard for banks and lenders that operate in this area.

Tax Credit

For a transferable tax credit, let's apply the same principle from our previous example of cash-flowing a tax rebate.

It should work in the same way but with the additional steps that we have already discussed.

Let's assume the same deal terms as before:

- 10% discount on the projected gross value

- 2.5% up-front fee

- 8% p.a. rate of interest

- 18-month term

- $10,000 legal fees

However, as this is a transferable tax credit, we also have some additional considerations to include here regarding the sale of the credit certificate.

Remember, the cash-flow numbers will be calculated on the final sale price of the credit, not the original value of the certificate.

So, let's say we find a broker who will sell our tax credit to one of their clients on the following terms:

- 90% sale price

- 1% broker fee

- $5,000 legal fees

Applying these terms to our figures, our calculations would look like this:

Projected Gross Value of Tax Credit		$1,700,000
End Sale Price	90%	$1,530,000
Broker Fee	1%	$15,300

Broker Legal Fees		$5,000
Net Value of Tax Credit After Sale		$1,509,700
Discount (in case of underspend)	10%	$150,970
Discounted Amount to be Cash-Flowed / Loan Facility Amount		$1,358,730
Up-Front Fee	2.5%	$33,968.25
Rate of Interest	8% p.a.	
Term	18 months	
Projected Interest		$163,047.60
Financier Legal Fees		$10,000
NET AMOUNT TO PRODUCTION		$1,151,714.15

So, in this case, according to these calculations, the bank will set up a loan facility of $1,358,730. This is also the number that they will be charging interest on.

The cash amount that they will be injecting into the production upfront is $1,151,714.15.

As you can see, this is a bit less than in our previous example with the tax rebate due to the additional costs of selling the tax credit certificate. But remember, that $1.15m might still be the difference between our film getting greenlit or not!

Many jurisdictions that offer a tax credit recognize that there are additional costs involved with this process so they have worked hard to make their incentives competitive with those locations that offer a tax rebate.

Don't be put off by the tax credit system just because of these extra steps. Do your calculations and comparisons, and the chances are that these tax credits will be well worth your consideration.

I should note that, in this example, the 10% discount has been applied to the net value of the tax credit <u>after</u> the sale. However, in some instances, I have also seen the discount applied to the projected gross value of the tax credit <u>before</u> the sale – in this case, that would be the original $1.7m number. This would change the figures slightly, so just be aware that different financiers have different ways of calculating this.

20. The Risks Of Cash-Flowing A Tax Incentive

For financiers, cash-flowing a tax incentive is generally considered to be one of the lowest-risk forms of investing in the entertainment industry.

Why?

Well, firstly, there are a number of checks and balances that protect the financier, such as the pre-certification process and the audit process.

All of these are put in place to keep everything regulated and transparent.

This is unlike other forms of debt financing such as the cash-flowing of pre-sales, where a financier must do a lot of research into the reputation of the distributor and their likelihood to honor and pay up on their commitment.

In that case, and particularly for gap financing, the financier is also faced with another extremely large and important variable: will the film or TV show you are making actually be any good? We discuss this in much more detail in another book in this series.

When cash-flowing a tax incentive, aside from ensuring that it does not contravene any content requirements to qualify, financiers do not need to concern themselves with the project's creative aspects at all. They don't need to read the script or worry about casting. It does not need to turn out well, achieve distribution, or be a success at the box-office. None of that is relevant here, which, for a financier, is good news!

Instead, the financier is faced with two main logistical risks:

- Will the tax incentive jurisdiction (city, state, region, or country) do what it says it will do?

- Will you (the production company and/or filmmaker) do what you say you will do?

These two risk factors will affect the financier's appetite to cash-flow your tax incentive, and will also define the fees they charge you.

Let's take a look at these risk factors...

21. Will The Tax Incentive Jurisdiction Do What It Says It Will Do?

A debt financier always has to look at who the counterparty is. In other words, who is the person or company that will eventually have to honor their commitment to pay, and how reliable are they?

As mentioned before, in other kinds of debt financing, this is extremely important. For example, when cash-flowing a pre-sale, the counterparty would be a distribution company, possibly from somewhere thousands of miles away on the other side of the globe.

While many distribution companies are extremely reputable, some of them are also notorious for not honoring their commitments and either re-negotiating or reneging completely once the film or TV show is delivered, as we discuss in another book in this series.

In that situation, therefore, the counterparty risk is relatively high.

However, in the case of cash-flowing a tax incentive, the counterparty is generally a public organization, typically a governmental body that is publicly funded. Except for certain extreme cases, this should mean that the counterparty risk is comparatively low.

Lower-Risk Counterparties

The last thing that a governmental organization ever wants is to be seen as dishonorable, untrustworthy, unprofessional or un-businesslike. Any whiff of this and companies will run a mile and not want to do business in their jurisdiction.

Most countries, states and even cities have a marketing budget specifically to attract businesses to their locations. More business means more employment, which means greater expenditure and more tax monies running through their economy.

So, they are very concerned to be seen as trustworthy and reliable at all times, as a place where people can do business comfortably without having to worry about whether their contracts and commitments will be honored.

From a financier's point of view, this is a good thing. It means that the organization providing the tax incentive will most likely do what it says it is going to do.

A tax incentive program is very clear and is public knowledge, so everybody knows exactly what will qualify, what their requirements are, and what the production company needs to do to get the tax rebate or credit once they have completed production.

For this reason – and with a few notable exceptions around the world! – the jurisdictions providing tax incentives are generally regarded as lower-risk counterparties.

So... There's No Risk?

However, 'lower-risk' doesn't equal 'no risk'.

For all their good intentions, things can go wrong with whomever is writing that final incentive check or certificate to you.

There have been numerous – and often well-publicized – examples of this over the years.

Some potential problems that can arise include:

Slow Payment

It's a governmental body. While that should make them a lower-risk counterparty overall, we all know that governmental bodies are often under-staffed and over-regulated. This can create a backlog in their workload and slow them down considerably.

On top of that, the bureaucratic process means that several people sometimes need to sign off on the same document. If one of these people is on vacation or takes an unexpected leave of absence, this can cause additional delays.

Because everything is publicly funded and requires total transparency, there are usually no short-cuts or ways around this. Additionally, if you find yourself in a busy period when things are moving slowly, for example around the end of the fiscal year when everyone is filing their taxes, this can cause an even greater lag in the process.

So, if they state that they will generate your tax incentive in 2-3 months, it's usually a good idea to allow for some kind of buffer, say another 1-2 months, on top of that.

This just gives you a margin of error and some room to maneuver if you need it.

The Jurisdiction Runs Out Of Money Or Is Under-Funded

In tough times of economic austerity and natural disasters, a lot can change in the months or years between the moment you are pre-certified and the moment you hand in your final books for an audit. Sometimes, power shifts, budgets change, money gets overspent in other areas, and these jurisdictions find themselves running short on funds.

We like to think it is rare, but it does happen.

And guess what – when it does happen, paying a tax rebate of millions of dollars to 'rich Hollywood producers' for the films they have just made falls way down the priority list. For the limited public funds that are available, production tax incentives will usually lag behind the needs of the local population (who are also local voters), which may require basic services such as welfare and education.

Unfortunately, states and countries find their budgets stretched all the time and are constantly having to juggle and balance their books to make everything work.

If this happens, it is still likely that the location will pay up eventually and honor their commitment to you, especially if you are already pre-certified and in their system. However, this will only be once they have sufficient funds to do so, which could be a while.

Until then, you just have to sit and wait patiently, and so does your financier. Suing a bankrupt state isn't going to do you much good. Trouble is, you are still paying a monthly rate of interest while you wait, one that may have increased significantly once the term of your loan has expired.

While some financiers may be sympathetic to your cause and work out a deal with you, others may not. This could result in you incurring a whopping interest rate increase as a penalty, which could disturb your entire recoupment waterfall and severely affect your other investors' chances of recouping their money.

For this reason, and although still fairly rare, a jurisdiction running out of money can be a big problem for all concerned.

A Change In The Tax Incentive Program

Tax incentive programs are constantly being introduced, changed, updated, renewed, or abolished in locations around the world.

This can sometimes happen without warning and without any obligation on the part of the organization that is overseeing it.

If this happens, once again, most jurisdictions will honor a commitment that was previously made even if, by the time you finish production and hand in your books, the legislation has changed or even disappeared.

This is another advantage of a location with a pre-certification requirement. A pre-certification agreement could place a legal obligation on that jurisdiction, which should protect you.

However, there still remains the possibility of the rug being pulled from underneath you when you are halfway through production, particularly in locations that may have less established film or TV production industries.

Try to get as much official paperwork from the jurisdiction as possible in advance should you ever need to make a case as to why they should honor a commitment that you had been counting on.

Recapture

This has become less of a concern in recent years but is still worth mentioning.

Referred to by a variety of terms, 'recapture' alludes to the possibility that a jurisdiction could change its laws at a future time and retroactively annul the tax incentive that they had already granted, even if some years later or transferred to another user.

This could also refer to an additional audit that takes place once the tax incentive has already been issued and notices a discrepancy in the numbers.

This is extremely rare. In certain US states where this had been a concern, it has generally been addressed and resolved by carefully-worded and updated legislation.

However, there was a time when it was such a concern that, even though the possibility was very remote, some financiers would not cash-flow tax incentives in certain locations where the possibility simply existed.

While this shouldn't be anything to be too concerned about, in jurisdictions where the tax incentive program might be new and relatively untested, it is always worth checking to ensure that this will not impede you.

Newer Programs

Perhaps as a combination of all the risks just mentioned, financiers generally feel less comfortable with newer tax incentive programs that have only recently been established and are still untried.

With a tax incentive program that has been around for years, financiers feel confident that the governing bodies have dealt with any teething problems, ironed out any creases, resolved any issues, and now have a well-oiled and smooth-running machine managed by people who know what they are doing and can reliably churn out tax incentives with minimal obstacles.

Newer programs may sound flashier and more beneficial, but financiers may be wary of them facing one or more of the issues mentioned here. This might cause them to impose a larger discount or higher fees to offset any increased risk that they might perceive.

There's something to be said for going with the old tried and tested programs.

However, this shouldn't stop you embracing newer programs that may offer more benefits. You just need to be aware of some of the risk factors as well. Your financier certainly will be...

22. Will You Do What You Say You Will Do?

The risks associated with the tax incentive jurisdictions usually present a far smaller concern to the financiers than whether the production company will fulfill its obligations.

One of the largest concerns is that a producer will fail to fulfill all the local requirements, as we discussed earlier. If, for example, a production needed to be pre-certified or hit a minimum spend requirement but didn't realize this until the production had been completed, that could stop the jurisdiction from issuing a check or certificate.

However, such risks are usually quite location-specific. Hopefully, the bank or financier that is cash-flowing your tax incentive will have their own experts on hand to ensure that these criteria are met. It is in your interests to work with them and ensure that you meet all the necessary requirements.

There are, however, a number of risks that are far outside of their control. This is why financiers tend to choose the producers and filmmakers to whom they lend very carefully indeed.

Some of the main risks associated with the production company's performance include the following:

Production Schedule

When cash-flowing your incentive, the term of your loan is calculated primarily on your production schedule, as well as the turnaround time of the tax incentive.

So, for example, if a certain US state claims that they generally issue a rebate check within 3 months of receiving the fully audited books, you might agree to a loan term of 12 months with your financier. This would give you time to close the financing, produce your show, audit your books, and then wait to receive your tax incentive.

If things go smoothly, that 12-month term should be sufficient.

However, we all know that things can go wrong and delays can happen. If there is a significant stoppage during either pre-production or principal photography, or even during post-production (if that is taking place in that jurisdiction), that could have a knock-on effect and significantly delay the date on which you receive that tax incentive.

If you are shooting in a location where you need to provide a copy of the finished film or TV show, problems in post-production could seriously affect this, even if they don't occur in that jurisdiction.

As we already know, if you go over your loan term, you could incur serious penalties and an increased rate of interest.

While you might think that the financier would be happy about this, believe me, most of the time they are not. Increased interest and penalty fees means that a production is having financial difficulties, which affects them as much as it affects you.

Most financiers would much prefer to see their loan repaid on time, along with their fees and interest, and to have that capital back in the bank so that they can re-invest it into another project.

Selecting a competent producer that has a track record of sticking to their production schedule and not incurring delays is therefore very important to a financier.

Filing The Books Correctly

Even once you've finished production and are ready to complete the tax incentive process, the financier needs to be sure that you and your accountants have filed all your books correctly and then submitted all your numbers in the proper fashion.

If your books are examined or audited by the local authorities and a major discrepancy shows up – even an innocent one – this can affect the turnaround time significantly for them to issue the tax incentive.

If your production team has not kept every single receipt and invoice, or they have filed something incorrectly or not dealt with certain expenses in the correct manner, this can add weeks to the audit process and push everything back.

So, a good producer should oversee this process every step of the way to ensure that everything is handled with diligence and care. It's going to make life a lot easier once you submit your books.

Underspend

The possibility of an underspend might be the most common concern a financier has in cash-flowing a tax incentive.

It's also the one that is least predictable, even for a great producer. **For all your thorough research, preparation and informed estimations, until you actually arrive in a location and begin to crew up and rent equipment, you simply cannot tell with absolute certainty whether every person or every item that you intended to hire locally will be available.**

Inevitably, the production may incur unforeseen expenses with the need to bring in people or equipment from outside.

While you should have a contingency in your budget to account for these additional expenses, this could severely impact the amount of the qualifying spend that you had predicted.

You might have been planning to rent a certain camera from a local vendor only to turn up and find that they rented out their last one to another production. You may have had a commitment from a local gaffer or grip who leaves you in the lurch a week before production to join a studio movie that is also shooting in the area.

In either of these circumstances, you may find that the only viable replacement must be brought in from another state or country. That means that their cost or salary might not be included in the qualifying spend any more, which will decrease the amount of your final tax incentive.

If you have borrowed $1m secured against a tax incentive based on your budgeted projections, but only receive a tax credit of $800,000 due to a local underspend, that is a major problem for both you and your financier. You will have to find that remaining $200,000 from somewhere else to pay off your loan.

This is the primary reason that the financier may place a discount in their calculations when creating your loan facility, and also why they will likely insist on hiring an independent analyst to make some conservative assumptions on their behalf.

It's not a personal insult to you as a producer or filmmaker. Underspend is a common occurrence and is sometimes extremely difficult to avoid, especially on larger productions that require a lot of equipment and crew.

Unfinished Production

It's every producer's nightmare: something catastrophic happens halfway through filming and, for whatever reason, you simply can't put the production back together and have to shut it down.

It may be that you have budgeted incorrectly and have run out of money. Perhaps one of the actors or the director became sick and had to bail out and couldn't be replaced. Perhaps the weather changed and made it impossible for you to complete photography.

There are a million things that can go wrong and cause a production to shut down. It happens very rarely, but not never. Again, it can be very difficult to predict.

This can have obvious and dire consequences for a financier cash-flowing a tax incentive.

If the production closes down early, then it won't spend the money that had been foreseen. This leads to a very severe underspend.

Some locations will still generate a tax incentive for the money that the production has already spent there, even if the film or TV show is not completed. In this case, there will at least be some kind of tax rebate or credit to work with, albeit a fraction of what had been foreseen.

However, some locations might not grant you any kind of incentive if there is no finished product.

Remember how some of them will want to see a logo or credit at the end of the final film or TV show?

Well, that might be an obligation that you can no longer fulfill, which spells deep trouble for your financier even if you have already started spending money in that location.

Fortunately, there are measures that can be taken to offset some of the risk of an unfinished production. The two main ones are:

- An insurance policy

- A completion bond

An insurance policy is self-explanatory. Just like any other kind of insurance policy, you would file a claim and the insurance company should cover you for some or all of the costs incurred directly as a result of the accident that has caused you to shut down production, provided that your policy covers this.

This would obviously <u>not</u> apply if the production simply ran out of money! However, other accidents or an 'Act of God' may be covered.

However, an insurance policy is mainly a stopgap measure that will tide you over for any significant delays in production. It won't compensate for the lack of local spend that had been predicted, and it won't remedy the situation effectively in case of a total shutdown.

That is where a completion bond comes in.

Some producers may not be familiar with a completion bond. Almost every traditional debt financier out there, whether cash-flowing tax incentives or pre-sales, or providing gap financing, will want to see a completion bond in place before they finalize your loan.

The completion bond guarantees that your production will be finished one way or another. It is far from ideal – there is still likely to be a significant underspend that will produce a greatly decreased tax incentive. But it will at least get the job done.

Let's look at this in a little more detail ...

23. Completion Bond

Many banks and financiers will want a completion bond (sometimes known as a 'completion guarantee') to be in place when cash-flowing a tax incentive, as well as when providing other forms of debt financing.

What Is A Completion Bond?

A completion bond comes from an external company that provides a guarantee that a film or TV show will be completed and delivered in the event that the production company is unable to fulfill its duties.

This will be as close to the original schedule and budget as possible but, in reality, sometimes just getting the project completed at all is a miracle under these circumstances.

You therefore need to have realistic expectations of how the project will look, both financially and creatively, if the completion bond is called upon. Using it is very much a last resort.

Consider a completion bond a rather drastic form of insurance for use in a worst-case scenario.

Some producers resent the obligation to obtain and pay for a completion bond, but it can be a deal-breaker when looking for debt financing, including the cash-flowing of a tax incentive.

A completion bond gives the financier (and all your other investors) comfort that the production will be finished and a tax incentive will be generated – somehow, by someone – to give them a chance of recouping their investment.

Who Can Issue A Completion Bond?

A completion bond is generally issued by a specialized bond company.

On their staff, you will find a mixture of financing and production expertise. This will include some who understand the nuances of putting a production together and the day-to-day demands of life on set, as well as others who can read and break down a budget. Others still will understand how financing is put together.

Whatever kind of production and finance plan you have, the bond company should be familiar with it and should be able to work with you.

Collectively, the bond company will examine your books, your budget and your cash-flow schedule (among many other details) to ensure that your goals are realistic and to regulate your spending activity.

They will also require regular reporting throughout the production to ensure that it is not going over-budget. They are legally on the hook if it does, so they will be very strict about this.

If, for any reason, the project runs out of funding during the production or even post-production process, the bond company can legally step in and 'take over'. This means that they can and must finish the production using their own funds.

That provides a great sense of security to financiers and filmmakers alike, knowing that, whatever happens, there will be a finished product.

But remember, that may end up being a very different no-frills version of the film or TV show that you originally set out to make, and you and your investors are entirely in their hands.

They might be able to fire any member of the crew – including the director, line producer and anyone else – and hire their own people in their place.

Before production, they will also go over most of the main crew, particularly the HOD's, to make sure that they are 'bondable'. In other words, they need to know that the producers, director, line producer and others have a track record and the ability to bring the project in on time and on budget.

Having the bond company finish your project is a last resort for all concerned. The bond company doesn't want to have to do it, and you don't want to have to call them in on it.

How Much Does A Completion Bond Cost... And Is It Worth It?

For this service, you can expect to pay the bond company a fee, which will usually be calculated as a percentage of your budget.

As always, this could be higher or lower depending on the size of the production, the company you are working with, the complexities of your financing, and several other factors. Generally, I would expect to see this around the 3% mark, but this can vary wildly with the market.

3% of your budget may not sound like much but it can add up to tens or even hundreds of thousands of dollars. For an independent production, this can be a significant amount of money, one that is not always easy to raise.

The debate over whether a completion bond is worth the cost for your production is a bigger issue.

Smaller films often do not have a completion bond. For many producers with lower-budget independent features, the cost is simply too much and becomes prohibitive when putting together their budget and financing.

Such a film might be fully funded by equity financing. If the equity financiers feel comfortable with the cash-flow situation in front of them, they will likely forego the extra expense of a completion bond and instead work to ensure that everything goes according to plan.

If something were to go wrong with the financing and the production suddenly runs out of money, they may simply be able to put their hands in their pockets to provide that extra financing themselves to complete the project.

But generally, larger independent productions of a few million dollars or more do tend to have a completion bond, particularly if they are looking to work with a debt financier to cash-flow their tax incentive or any other kind of collateral, such as pre-sales.

In these cases, the extra cost of the completion bond is offset by the injection of cash that they will gain from such debt financing, so it becomes worth the expense.

Even if there is no debt financing involved, higher-budget productions often still have a completion bond. There is just so much money at stake that some investors will get nervous at the lack of security surrounding their investment.

Having a completion bond in place, particularly with the additional regulations provided by a bond company during pre-production and production itself, offers investors that extra reassurance in case things go wrong. The bond company also brings additional benefits that some investors appreciate, such as regulating cashflow and acting as an independent body to flag up any irregularities during the production process.

Ultimately, if having a completion bond is a deal-breaker in your efforts to obtain additional funding by cash-flowing your tax incentive, you may be left with no choice.

Alternatives To A Completion Bond

Fortunately, some newer lenders and financiers have appeared that may be willing to cash-flow a tax incentive even without a completion bond in place.

They have come up with innovative ways to offset part of the risk of their investment.

For example, they may only provide funding on a weekly basis once they have checked your books from the previous week of production to ensure that you are spending what you had predicted. That way, if there is a sudden cash-flow crisis, they can react to that quickly without having to put the entire loan amount at risk.

Other financiers might accept some other form of completion guarantee, perhaps from one of your investors or another source. While not an official completion bond company, a wealthy investor might give a legally-binding commitment that they will provide the necessary funds to get the production finished, whatever the cost may be.

They may be required to put a certain amount of funds in escrow, hopefully to sit there unused. But if the debt financier feels confident in their ability to rescue the production if necessary, they may accept this instead of a completion bond.

Remember though, where there is added risk, there may be additional cost. If a debt financier is cash-flowing your incentive, the lack of a traditional completion bond may present added risk to them, which could drive up their fees and interest rate.

If you really can't afford a completion bond, go out and see whether any financiers or lenders would be willing to work with you on an equivalent basis like this. Competition is fierce out there, so you might just find someone who will take a chance on you or have another way to get comfortable with this scenario.

Be sure to shop around, speak to different lenders and financiers to see what their requirements are, and then go and grab the best deal for you and your production!

PART FOUR

24. Shooting In A Location That Does Not Have A Tax Incentive

So, after reading all this, why would anyone ever shoot in a location that does <u>not</u> offer a tax incentive?

Weighing Up The Costs Versus The Benefits

A lot of great movies and TV shows do still get shot without the aid of tax incentives.

For each of these productions, the producers probably considered the possibilities of shooting in Louisiana or New Mexico, Hungary or Canada, but ultimately found that the additional costs of shooting there actually outweighed the benefits of the tax incentive program.

And <u>that</u> is the essential balance that you must always weigh up.

When the costs start to outweigh the benefits, moving your production to a new shooting location simply for the tax incentive might not be the best decision. You should always consider all the incentives on offer, but don't <u>chase</u> an incentive if it's not the right fit for your project.

There are a few good reasons why shooting in a location that does <u>not</u> have a tax incentive might, after careful analysis, still be the best option for your production.

These can include:

Production Costs

Production is an expensive business, and the cost of producing content can vary wildly from city to city, state to state, and country to country.

Sometimes, you might find the perfect location to shoot your project, fitting every one of your creative needs. That location might not have a tax incentive, but its costs might be 50% cheaper than shooting somewhere that does.

In those circumstances, even a large rebate check probably wouldn't match the benefits that you could achieve by shooting in a location where your budget has been halved and your savings are so significant.

Sometimes, you might find locations that do not have a tax incentive but nonetheless have a very proactive film commission. They probably recognize that their lack of incentives makes them less competitive in the market to attract productions, so they come up with other innovative ways to make it worth your while.

They will find ways to cut your costs, maybe by helping you find free locations, offering permits for free, or utilizing partnerships with local services such as hotels and restaurants to cut your budget down.

In this way, some places can subsidize their lack of a tax incentive by reducing your production costs instead, and thereby making themselves a great and cost-effective shooting location for certain types of productions.

Local Infrastructure And Favors

If you are from a location where you have a great network and infrastructure, this can sometimes be more valuable than any tax incentive.

Some producers have made very successful careers for themselves based in non-traditional shooting locations outside of the more recognized creative hubs. Having worked in these places for many years, they now have an established network of local cast and crew that they can call upon, along with an unbeatable knowledge of their locale and all aspects of shooting there.

Having a local infrastructure can allow you to produce content freely and cheaply, and to call on favors in times of need to bring down production costs. This can add huge value to a production, particularly when the budget is small and there is not much financing available.

Even if you could potentially re-locate to a place with a tax incentive program, the experience might not be as good and the production value might not be as high. Most importantly, it may not even be cost-effective in comparison.

If you can use your local contacts to gain access to free locations or skilled friends who will work on your production for a fraction of their regular fees, where you might have access to accommodations to put up crew members instead of a hotel, or maybe even connect with a restaurant that can provide the production's catering, these could all cut down production costs in a way that could not be matched by a tax incentive.

Balancing the costs against the benefits of shooting in a tax incentive location can sometimes come down to seemingly small details like these.

Specific Location

We mentioned this earlier in the book but it bears repeating: **the tax incentive should never be at the expense of the creative**.

If your project calls for a specific location, you have two options:

1) Shoot in that specific location

2) Re-create that location somewhere else

Of course, wherever possible, you will want to go with the first option and shoot at that specific location.

Now, if that location is in a place that doesn't have a tax incentive, you can examine the costs of re-creating it somewhere that does. If it is somewhere that is easy to re-create, then this can still be a great option.

This happens all the time! Countless places around the world have doubled for New York or Los Angeles and you'd never know due to the fantastic production design and meticulous attention to detail, combined with strategically-placed B-roll and pick-up shots in the required location.

But say your project takes place, for example, in and around the Las Vegas Strip. Obviously, you could re-create certain scenes and moments in another location, but the costs of building an entire casino floor or re-creating the exteriors of the iconic Strip somewhere else might simply be too prohibitive for any production, whilst also lacking the authenticity and production value that you really need.

It's always a good idea to see how much you can fake or re-imagine somewhere else. But if a specific location is intrinsic to your project creatively then you may simply have to bite the bullet and shoot there, tax incentive or not.

Travel Costs

When shooting outside a major production hub, you will almost always incur significant travel costs to bring in your essential cast and crew members.

By travel costs, I am not simply referring to the transportation itself (which is expensive enough), but also to expenses related to accommodation, meals, additional transport, per diems, and many other items.

These travel costs can really add up, particularly when you are on a budget. You may also be required to provide a minimum standard of transport or accommodation by an actor or crew member's union.

A chunk of these expenses should be covered by the tax incentive in the location that you are traveling to. But there's no getting around the fact that your budget will increase significantly.

Once again, it is important to be aware of just how much it will cost to set your production up somewhere new.

If you were able to shoot in a location where the talent and crew is already based, even if that location does not have a tax incentive, you may still end up saving money by not having to travel them all out and incur the expenses that go with that.

Securing The Talent

Having a great crew behind the camera is extremely important but ultimately, from both a critical and commercial standpoint, the actors that you have in front of the camera can define the success (or lack of it) of your film or TV show.

Wherever you end up shooting, you will be able to find crew somehow, either locally or by bringing them in.

The talent, however, is a tougher nut to crack, and often producers find that the demands of their talent play a significant role when choosing their location.

Imagine you have a low-budget indie film and you have managed to attract a big star to be a part of it. That's great! This will help you to secure financing and give you a much better shot at getting distribution.

The star might want to be part of this small movie even though they are not being paid very much money. Why? Maybe they think it will be a festival film or they could win an award with it, maybe it's about an issue they are really interested in... It could be any number of reasons.

However, that doesn't necessarily mean that they will want to spend a month shooting in a distant location that they are not familiar with, living out of a hotel room, far away from their home and family, just so that you can shoot in a location with a tax incentive.

Some stars will simply pull out of the project. However much they may want to do it, spending time away from home and away from their daily lives is simply too great a burden to them unless they are being paid a huge salary.

Others may agree to do it, but you will still have to meet some of their demands.

This could be expensive. They will need first-class tickets and top hotels wherever they stay, and they may want to fly out their partner, their kids, a nanny, a tutor, a dog, or whatever else they need around them to keep them happy (and you definitely want to keep them happy!).

They might want to bring their own stylist, assistant, personal trainer, or anyone else they want to have with them, and the production will have to foot the bill for all these additional people, as well as their accommodation and travel.

Some of these expenses might qualify for the tax incentive where you are shooting, but some might not. Either way, your budget is ballooning due to the costs associated with your new location. It's starting to look like more trouble than it's worth...

In this scenario, the question remains: would you be better off shooting in a place where the star is based? They would be happy and comfortable, surrounded by their usual home comforts. The production would then not have to incur any of these additional costs, even though this star might live in Los Angeles and you may not be able to secure the California tax incentive.

As always, it's a question of numbers, weighing up the costs against the benefits. Each project has its own set of circumstances, so remain flexible and open to all options, and see what works best for you.

25. Other Potential Benefits Of A Location

Aside from all the official tax incentives, it's always a good idea to get to know the local film commission (or equivalent) wherever you are shooting as far in advance as possible.

Some places offer a wide variety of additional benefits to help attract your production to their location. Depending on how big your production is, and how aggressive that particular film commission can be, this can be really helpful when making your final decision.

The film commission could assist you in saving money or even finding some additional financing.

Remember to do as much research as possible. Sometimes you might find a country that offers a tax incentive, but the states or regions within that country might have additional benefits they can offer you on top of that.

Within those states or regions, there may be individual cities that can throw in a little extra to give you even more of an incentive. And if they can't top up the incentive, perhaps they could help you find free locations or offer free permits, as we mentioned previously. Every little thing can make a difference.

Never be ashamed to ask what they can do for you. After all, they need you and your business.

It's impossible to cover every kind of additional benefit available here, but I will share a few things to look out for from my experience that may help you in addition to a tax incentive.

These include:

Costs And Attitude

We've noted this already but it's worth pointing out again: some of these non-traditional shooting locations are simply much cheaper places to live and do business.

The popularity of some of the traditional production hubs such as Los Angeles, New York and London has led to them becoming extremely expensive cities in which to operate. Whether you need hotels, restaurants, transportation, or virtually anything else, you will generally be paying top dollar.

Some of these non-traditional shooting locations are not regarded as typical tourist destinations or international business hubs. The costs of living and working there can be significantly cheaper, which could save you a lot of money in your budget.

You may also find the local population there far more friendly and excited about the idea of a production taking place there.

In Hollywood, people are very used to seeing movies and TV shows being shot on their doorstep, and no longer view it as much of a big deal. If anything, it can become quite an annoyance, and an invasion into their everyday lives.

However, in other parts of the world, people are often far more excited at the prospect of being part of the entertainment system. They may be more friendly, and far more willing to accommodate you and your production's needs than you would find back home.

Benefits For Writers And Directors

It is crucial for writers and directors in particular to get to know their local film commissions and their local industry as a whole.

If a writer is aware that a certain region has an attractive tax incentive program, they can use that knowledge to set a project there and encourage production in a financially-beneficial area. The local film commission will likely welcome such creative efforts as an organic way to promote their region and its film industry, and they may be able to offer significant help in getting the project launched.

Certain regions may have incentives in place specifically to support local talent, even if a project is at a very early stage.

These can include financial incentives to help with your project, as well as opportunities for you to showcase your talent and meet local investors.

In fact, they may support you and your project even if you don't ultimately shoot in their location. It's still beneficial for them to have a homegrown success story, and may reflect well on them as a film commission.

Contact your local film commission, whether that is at country, state, county, or even city level, and see what support they may be able to offer you.

Leave no stone unturned, and don't leave any money on the table!

Grants

Some locations offer a variety of grants to help promote their region. These usually tend to be development grants for local writers that they are banking on to help put their location on the map.

This may not be a huge amount of money but, for an aspiring filmmaker with a project in development, it can be a game-changer.

Other kinds of grants might also be available to any number of people.

If you are from a social or ethnic group that is traditionally regarded as a 'minority' (such as African-Americans or LGBTQ), there may be grants available specifically for you. Many areas will look to become as diverse as possible and encourage a new generation of local filmmakers from these traditionally underrepresented groups of filmmakers.

These regions generally know what big business film and TV production can be for them so they may be able to invest these grants very aggressively in local filmmakers at a grassroots level and establish a relationship with them from an early stage.

Subsidies

Some locations may have their own funds that they can invest into your project on top of the tax incentive, possibly as equity. This usually isn't a lot but, again, even small amounts can make a huge difference as you put your financing together.

Sometimes these investments will recoup in a junior equity position behind your primary investors, which makes these funds even more user-friendly for producers and financiers.

These funds might be administered by the film commissions themselves, or they might be separately-managed funds using public or private money. Again, these funds would likely have the intention of promoting local talent and boosting the local entertainment industry and, consequently, the local economy overall.

So, these kinds of subsidies will almost always be based on a certain amount of money or time being spent in their region or being used to promote it in some way.

Always remember to check what conditions might be attached to such funds, and how much these might then tie you into shooting in that location and any requirements you may have to fulfill.

The worst thing would be if you were counting on this investment only to find that, in fact, you hadn't followed the rules and will not receive the money you were expecting.

Remember to check with the local film commission and ask whether there is any additional financial support that they can offer you.

Studios As Investors

In some of these non-traditional locations in particular, investors sometimes put large amounts of money into an expensive studio or post-production facility only to find that, by the time they have finished construction, their local tax incentive program has changed or a neighboring location has come up with something even better.

So, you might find that these facilities will offer you additional funding or benefits to come and shoot or do your post-production there.

The local film commission should know whether any of these facilities can offer you something extra.

Alternatively, they might be able to offer you some 'services-in-kind', whereby they will charge you a heavily discounted rate for their services and, in return, they will take an equity position to recoup their investment on the back-end. This can save you a lot of money from your budget. We discuss services-in-kind in more detail in another book in this series about equity investments.

Studios are something that cannot be moved or re-located depending on a tax incentive. You have to go to them, and they will want to fill their sound stages and editing suites.

So, it's always worth asking around the local facilities and seeing whether they can offer you any additional benefits to working with them.

Location Scouting

Most locations understand that the best way to sell you on shooting there is to bring you over and impress you in person. This is especially the case for less conventional locations.

If they think that you are a serious filmmaker and believe that you are genuine about shooting in their location, they may be willing to fly you out for a location scout and cover some of your costs for a few days, including hotels, meals and transport.

This can save you a lot of money, particularly as it can be tough to find development financing (which is traditionally used for location scouts) for independent projects.

Investment Vehicles

Certain locations offer tax-efficient structures that encourage investment in that region. Filmmakers can use these structures as a way of enticing local equity investors to put money into their productions.

This is usually done at a federal level (for a country, rather than a state or a city) and are government-backed vehicles to encourage economic growth in the entertainment industry.

By offering some kind of tax relief to investors, they are factoring against the potential downside of investing in film and TV production, which is sometimes viewed as a more risky investment compared to certain other asset classes such as property or the stock market.

In other words, they offer potential investors a tax benefit. This should make providing funding to the entertainment industry more attractive to them. In some places, they can also claim some tax relief to cushion any losses on their investment.

These are often very intricate structures that require more attention than can be offered in this book. However, if you are looking for innovative ways to raise money, it is always worth investigating whether any of these structures are available in the shooting location of your choice.

If such a structure is available, <u>always</u> consult with your accountants or other licensed financial professionals who will be able to advise you on how to take advantage of these structures in order to raise financing.

The investors themselves should also take the necessary legal and financial advice from qualified professionals.

Remember, these will be governmental structures that are open to public scrutiny, so it is vitally important to do everything by the book and with qualified professionals who are familiar with the local legislation.

Two recent examples of these kinds of structures that many filmmakers have taken advantage of are:

- Section 181 (US)

    o This recent legislation in the US allowed certain investors in specific types of productions to deduct their appropriate expenditures when filing their taxes

- EIS ('Enterprise Investment Scheme') (UK)

    o This recent legislation in the UK allowed investors in certain types of productions (or production funds) to obtain 30% upfront income tax relief on the first £1m of their investment, as well as tax relief from any investment losses

Now, these are just two examples of what I am referring to as 'investment vehicles'. This is not designed to be tax or investment advice. These examples are used here for illustrative purposes only. Please note that new legislation gets enacted all the time and old rules get discarded, so, by the time you read this, these examples may or may not still be valid. Always check beforehand as this can be very changeable!

If this doesn't make much sense to you, don't worry. In any country where such investment vehicles and structures exist, there will likely be an established infrastructure of qualified people that can advise you on the best way to take advantage of whatever is on offer.

The point is this: there may be structures that you can take advantage of in certain places that can help you raise money for your production.

Again, ask all the questions you can – any extra incentive that you can offer an investor could make a big difference!

International Co-Productions

This is another rather complicated area that could be a book in itself!

For now, I at least want to make you aware of international co-productions and the opportunities that they can bring.

Certain countries have international co-production treaties that allow a production to take advantage of some or all of the tax incentives in more than one location. Such a treaty might actually transcend the minimum requirements that each country has if structured in the right way.

It may also allow a production to be split equally between more than one country, or possibly to have the majority of production in one country and then certain other elements (such as exterior shooting, B-roll, or even post-production) in another and still take advantage of some of the benefits on offer.

In fact, it is not uncommon to see productions set up as official co-productions between two, three, or even more countries! This is a well-established system that is there to help you. In this scenario, double-dipping on more than one tax incentive is perfectly acceptable. You will likely need to work with a local production company in your co-production partner country to access these benefits.

However, you should note that, with international co-productions, you are dealing with two (or more) sets of rules, two sets of governmental procedures and bureaucracy, two different infrastructures, and two systems and cultures that might work at very different paces.

Setting your production up in this way can be very beneficial in the long run but it can be a lot of work and, for lower-budget films in particular, sometimes the benefit does not justify the costs and effort that go into making it happen. There will also still be minimum requirements that you will have to meet in your co-production structure, budget and financing.

There are also regulations in place in each place that generally prevent you from introducing country after country after country into a co-production agreement that will end up fully funding your project through public subsidies. So, even if you do plan to take advantage of one of these co-production treaties, it's important to have realistic expectations of what you can get out of this.

Additionally, please note that, at the time of writing, the US does not have any official co-production treaties with any other countries. So, if you are planning a US-based shoot, it is very unlikely that you will be able to involve another country and make it an official international co-production. However, do check whether this is still the case as you go into production.

Again, the point of bringing this up here isn't to offer a comprehensive study on international co-productions right now, but rather to make you aware of them so that you can at least investigate the possibilities if they present themselves.

26. The Final Word

Choosing the right location for your project can be complicated, but doing it in the right way can bring major benefits that will help you get your film or TV show into production!

Taking advantage of a location's tax incentive program has now become an essential part of the financing and production process, whether you're a small independent company or a major studio.

Remember, don't leave money on the table!

I hope that this book has helped you to understand some of the important decisions that go into selecting the right location and tax incentive program for you, and how these decisions can actually help you get your project funded.

As with most things in life, and especially in production, nobody knows everything and this is an ongoing process and ever-evolving marketplace. But once you have grasped the principles discussed in this book, you can feel confident when going out and choosing a location that you are armed with the best possible knowledge to make the right decision for your production.

Happy filmmaking!

AUTHOR'S NOTE

Thank you for reading my book on Tax Incentives! I hope you found it useful, and that it helps propel your next film or TV project to success.

I remember when I first arrived in Hollywood. Just like you, I was full of dreams and ambitions, ready to work hard and make great content. But I found it really tough trying to figure out how films and TV shows actually got selected, financed, and produced.

That's why I'm sharing my experience of over twenty years and more than thirty film and TV titles with you now. I truly believe that this knowledge can make or break a career in the entertainment industry – it really is that important. **These books have been a labor of love for me.** They are the resources that I wish I'd had when I first arrived in Hollywood.

Your feedback means a lot to me. **I'd be really grateful if you would consider taking a minute to leave a review of this book.** Reviews make a huge difference for both authors and publishers, and they help to spread the word to other filmmakers who might appreciate this information.

Please also feel free to reach out and connect with me on social media or via The Film Finance Club. I love hearing from passionate filmmakers and learning what you are working on.

Happy filmmaking!

Ricky Margolis
Los Angeles, 2020

FURTHER INFORMATION

JOIN OUR MAILING LIST! Stay informed on new developments and further releases from the HOW THE HELL... team by visiting our website at www.howthehell.online.

For further information on film financing, including tips and information on our blog, please visit The Film Finance Club at www.thefilmfinanceclub.com.

For further information on Wunderfunkmaschine, or for consulting or partnership opportunities, please visit our website at www.wunderfunkmaschine.com.

You can get in touch with us via our website or on social media.

Other Books In This Series

HOW THE HELL... Do I Get My Film Financed?: Book Two: SALES & DISTRIBUTION : How The Sales And Distribution Process Can Help You Get Your Film Or TV Show Financed And Produced!

HOW THE HELL... Do I Get My Film Financed?: Book Three: EQUITY FINANCING : What Filmmakers Need To Know About Raising Equity & What Investors Need To Know About Investing It!

HOW THE HELL... Do I Get My Film Financed?: Book Four: BUSINESS PLAN : How To Create The Perfect Business Plan To Raise Funding For Your Film Or TV Show!

ABOUT THE AUTHOR

Ricky Margolis has over twenty years' experience in the entertainment industry. During that time, he has worked in a variety of positions at both large studios and boutique production companies.

He has gained extensive knowledge and expertise in a number of aspects of the industry, including production, finance, development, literary management, sales, distribution, and marketing.

Over the course of his career, Ricky has been involved in the production, finance, sales and/or distribution of over thirty titles, including films, TV shows, and web series.

Ricky also has experience in the financial services industry, with several years' experience in venture capital, business development, and startup funding.